LALIQUE

LALIQUE

TONY L MORTIMER

CHARTWELL
BOOKS. INC.

First published in Great Britain in 1989 by Pyramid, an imprint of the
Octopus Publishing Group,
Michelin House, 81 Fulham Road, London SW3 6RB

Above: *Detail from 'Phalenes'
(Butterflies) bowl. Circa 1929*

Title page: *'Deux figurines', a frosted
glass clock. Circa 1925. 37.5 cm $14\frac{3}{4}$ in*

This 1989 edition published by
CHARTWELL BOOKS, INC
A Division of BOOK SALES, INC.
110 Enterprise Avenue, Secaucus, New Jersey 07094

© Octopus Books Limited 1989

ISBN 1–55521 293–X

10 9 8 7 6 5 4 3 2 1 First American Edition

Produced by Mandarin Offset
Printed and bound in Hong Kong

CONTENTS

'Tournesol' (Sunflowers) vase. Height 12 cm 4¾ in

6

INTRODUCTION

René Lalique was one of those rare individuals — one of the small handful of artists whose ability and versatility is such that they achieve great success in more than one field. Lalique was a master jeweller who created some of the most dazzling and original pieces ever seen, who later became an inspired glass-maker with a highly developed business sense, and an interior decorator and exhibition designer, second to none. His career embraced the curvilinear art nouveau and the geometric art deco styles, and his clientele ranged from multi-millionaires and the socialites and leading actresses of the belle époque to members of the middle class with modest incomes.

The beginnings of the artistic revival which became internationally known as art nouveau may be traced to the Great Exhibition of 1851 at the Crystal Palace in London. This monumental event, originally the brainchild of Prince Albert, was housed in a giant building of iron and glass which was revolutionary in its design. The exhibits mainly consisted of artefacts which were on the one hand products of the industrial revolution and on the other essentially imitations of established works of art in the classical, baroque and rococo styles, and little more than mindless repetitions of revived and established trends, designed to gratify the needs of the *nouveaux riches*, whose numbers were increasing as a result of industrialization. The age of the ma-

chine was doing nothing to encourage individual artistic creativity.

Following the Great Exhibition of 1851 a movement of rebellion began against the derivative, 'safe' art forms beloved of Victorian manufacturers. A new mode of craftsmanship was required, one which was completely original in concept and methods of manufacture. This new style, art nouveau, was to extend to every area of artistic creativity — architecture, textiles, carpets and wallpapers, furniture and jewellery, ceramics, metalwork and glass — and established itself not only in the countries of western Europe but in the United States as well. Its aim was to create articles of outstandingly beautiful design and craftsmanship, from a cathedral spire to a humble knife and fork, which were to be not only visually pleasing but functional as well.

The Arts and Crafts Movement was founded by one of the earliest exponents of art nouveau, William Morris, and various arts and crafts societies were established in the later decades of the 19th century. Unfortunately many of these were doomed to failure. Artefacts made by individual craftsmen were essentially more expensive than those mass-produced in factories and in many cases the Victorian middle-class clientele simply could not afford the prices of these new products. Nevertheless the foundations of this exciting modern art form soon became firmly established and began to spread throughout western Europe.

In 1862 Japanese art was exhibited for the first time in Paris, the acknowledged cultural capital of the western world. The style of oriental decoration amazed and delighted European and American connoisseurs. It had a profound effect upon the art nouveau artists and craftsmen and greatly influenced some of their designs which began to reflect the Japanese shapes and patterns. Cluttered Victorian rooms where every inch of available space was filled with memorabilia began to be seen and criticized for what they undoubtedly were – the dust-traps of a bygone age. How much better to have just one or two porcelain or pottery items on a mantelpiece, designed in the very best of taste and choice of colour, instead of perhaps as many as twenty pieces, all mass-produced, with little or no aesthetic appeal or value.

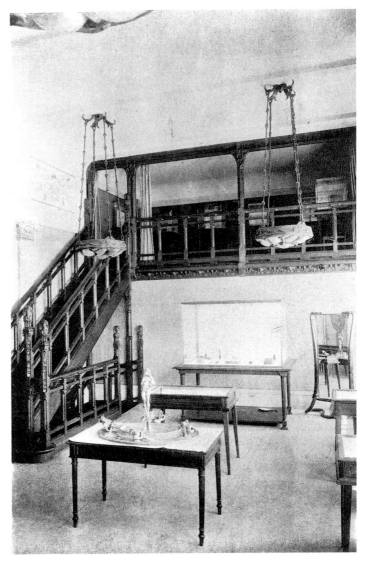

Opposite: *René Lalique in 1931. An oil painting by his daughter, Suzanne Lalique. A vase in the Albert design is on his left and a long stemmed goblet on his right*

Right: *The showroom at 40 Cours La Reine, illustrated in* L'Art Décoratif *in 1905. A colour picture of the silver centre piece on the table appears on page 43*

Although the prime instigators of the art nouveau movement were English, it was in France that the world's most creative artists were living at this time. It was natural, therefore, that the new art form should be christened in French as art nouveau, even though the French had called it 'le style Anglais' for some years.

The characteristics of art nouveau

What are the essential qualities of art nouveau design? Three distinct modes of decoration and shape, simultaneously asymmetrical and curvilinear, are most frequently used by exponents of this art form.

One hallmark of art nouveau is the female nude form which is nearly always elongated and almost always devoid of sexual features. Another is the use of motifs directly concerned with nature – animals, birds, flowers, trees and insects – these are also depicted in an elongated manner with sweeping, sinuous curves and tendrils. Particularly popular are the peacock and butterfly, with their iridescent colours reminiscent of Japanese art. Seaweed and leaves are also frequently featured, along with dragonflies, drooping sunflowers and lilies. Thirdly and by no means the least important is the curved line or tendril, flowing, bending, twisting and turning back on itself like a whiplash; sensuous in the extreme, described variously as 'women's hair, blown by the wind' the 'casual wispy smoke of a fire on a still day', or the 'waves of bounding sea surf'.

Art nouveau and Lalique

The apex of European art nouveau was reached at the Paris Exposition of 1900: the opulence and magnificence of the exhibits were in striking contrast with those at the Great Exhibition fifty years before. The many artists who expressed their talents in the art nouveau style have left behind them a reputation for brilliance which has been recognized as something quite unique by art connoisseurs. It was said of the most outstanding of them all: 'He ranks amongst the greatest figures in the history of art of all time and his so personal masterly touch, his exquisite imagination will excite the admiration of future elites'. These were the words of one of the world's greatest art collectors and patrons, Calouste Sarkis Gulbenkian. He was referring to a man destined for immortality by his creation of objects of outstanding beauty and extraordinary design. This man was René Lalique.

Early years

René Lalique was born on 6 April 1860 in the rural environment of Ay, in the Département of Marne in France. Although his early childhood was spent in Paris he returned to the countryside as often as possible to gain inspiration for his creative genius. He went to school at the Lycée Turgot, near Vin-

Opposite: Brooch, circa 1900–2, depicting a kissing couple with flesh carved in ivory and hair of gold, entwined with blue enamel foliage and gold branches. Height 7.2 cm 3 in

cennes. He studied nature in its various forms and in his early teens was already selling paintings of flowers and insects on ivory plaques. His early artistic endeavours were recognized by his mother who apprenticed him at the age of sixteen to the Paris jeweller Louis Aucoc. He enrolled in the Ecole des Arts Décoratifs before beginning two years' study at Sydenham College on the outskirts of London, in 1878.

This period undoubtedly left its mark on Lalique, for English art was undergoing a renaissance at the time, with the Arts and Crafts Movement vibrantly alive, but little is known of how he spent his two years in England, except that he studied draughtsmanship. Sydenham College was geographically very close to the site of the Crystal Palace and the young man cannot have failed to be inspired by the proximity of this great exhibition centre.

Lalique's ambition was to become a leading jewellery designer and when he returned to Paris in 1880 he began a detailed study of jewellery manufacturing techniques. He also studied sculpture under Justin Lequien at the Ecole Bernard Palissy, which played another important part in his formative training. Palissy pottery dishes and moulds decorated in relief with realistically modelled plants, fishes, molluscs and reptiles, including snakes, lizards and

toads, may well have influenced Lalique in his use of naturalistic models bordering on the bizarre. It was while he was at the Palissy school, too, that he made his first designs for fabrics and wallpapers.

Lalique based most of his early jewellery work on traditional designs and materials, selling to the leading Parisian jewellery houses of Aucoc, Boucheron, Cartier and Destape. These pieces were usually diamond-set creations, always popular with the aristocracy. His real chance to experiment and follow up his innovatory ideas began when he took over a small workshop on the Place Gaillon from Jules Destape, who retired in 1885. This marked the beginning of Lalique's years of creative genius.

The beauty and unusual quality of Lalique jewellery are inherent in his designs. He sought to create the ideal without using expensive materials. His creations using less expensive metals, glass and semi-precious stones are as appealing as those made from gold, silver and precious stones.

In 1887 Lalique exhibited some of his new jewellery designs at the Exposition Nationale des Arts Industriels in Paris, an event which was organized concurrently with an exhibition of the French crown jewels at the Louvre. His designs began to be recognized as outstanding works of art, although some critics considered his forms 'decadent and too fantastic' and 'visually disturbing'. Many of his early jewellery pieces were revolutionary in concept and designed to shock: some of his insect creations, for example, were indeed frighteningly realistic.

Opposite: A gold, enamel and opal pendant, circa 1902–03, showing two peacocks facing each other, above flowering prunus branches. Height 9 cm $3\frac{1}{2}$ in

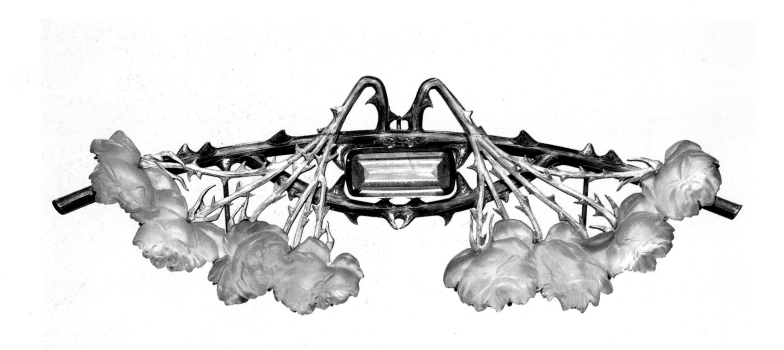

In 1890 Lalique was managing a small factory in the rue Thérèse in Paris which employed around thirty workmen. He married the daughter of the sculptor Auguste Ledru in this year and acquired the services of both his father-in-law and brother-in-law. At this time he was experimenting extensively with working in different materials of varying colour shades and his relatives assisted him in the carving of relief jewellery. Lalique's experiments with enamels and glass paved the way for his future art deco career.

Around 1892 Lalique secured the patronage of the great actress Sarah Bernhardt, known in Parisian circles as the 'Divine Sarah'. This proved a valuable commercial asset which immediately gained him an international reputation. He exhibited widely at the Salon de Paris and in 1897 was awarded the Légion d'Honneur. His reputation as a leading jeweller of the art nouveau movement was now established on a worldwide basis.

In 1902 he moved to a five-storey house at 40 Cours la Reine which he had had specially built. One of the outstandingly significant features of this building was the front doors which were made to

Above: *Openwork rose brooch, circa 1905–10, with full-blown blooms of moulded glass and stems of gold and opalescent enamel trailing over a central amethyst. H. 5.7 cm 2¼ in*

his own design, with glass panels which simulated pine branches with cones.

Lalique showed his work all over western Europe, with several exhibitions in London. In 1903 the Grafton Gallery mounted an exhibition devoted entirely to his work. Many of the 163 items on show were lent by Lalique's most important patron, the renowned Armenian multimillionaire businessman and art connoisseur, Calouste Gulbenkian, an ardent admirer who had the vision to recognize Lalique's artistic genius and had prudently purchased many of his works at previous shows.

Agnew's, the well-known Bond Street fine art gallery, held another very successful showing of Lalique's works in 1905, by which time his reputation was recognized by the very highest in society. It was in 1905, too, that Lalique opened his first retail establishment at 24 Place Vendôme in Paris. He enjoyed royal patronage, with Queen Alexandra acquiring some of his creations. As Princess of Wales she had enjoyed a reputation as a leader of fashion, and after Queen Victoria's death she began to create a style of dress which stressed the majesty of royalty, with fashionable clothes made in lighter colours. Jewels were no longer reserved for court occasions: Queen Alexandra began to wear daytime jewellery, stressing the femininity of fashion in her choice. Among the Lalique pieces she owned was a small gold triangular pendant featuring two swans upon a lake made in enamels set within a framework representing the outline of another swan, whose curved neck acted as an

Above: *Sarah Bernhardt, the great actress, whose patronage from the early 1890s helped to establish René Lalique's international reputation*

attachment for a gold chain. Another was a finely carved horn comb with overlaid decoration of the white-flowered chincherinchee lily.

Lalique's use of glass

By wearing Lalique's jewellery, Queen Alexandra confirmed his recognized status as a master craftsman, but René Lalique never allowed himself to rest upon his laurels. His mind was forever active, searching for the unusual and the unknown, and he experimented with many materials in his endeavours to create innovatory effects. His use of glass in particular was to win him universal acclaim. He had used glass successfully in many of his early creations, but by 1900 his jewellery was being copied and the market flooded with cheap imitations. Art nouveau was now on the wane and Lalique began to look for other ways in which to satisfy his artistic creativity. In 1902 he acquired a small workshop in Clairefontaine where he began to experiment in earnest with glass, using the process known as *cire perdue* or 'lost wax'. Some of the pieces resulting from these early experiments were exhibited at the Salon de Paris. In 1907 the *parfumeur* François Coty invited Lalique to design the labels for his scent bottles and it was not long before he was designing the bottles themselves. In 1909 he opened his own glassworks at Combs, called Verrerie de Combs la Ville, and was soon manufacturing a wide range of articles made from glass. This venture proved so successful that the factory had to be expanded and in 1918 he had a much larger glassworks, Verrerie

Above: *Light fitting in* cire perdue *glass, circa 1909–10. Width 32 cm 12½ in. Lalique continued to use the 'lost wax' technique until the late 1930s*

Opposite: *'Styx' flacon, 1910–13. 12 cm 4¾ in, with intaglio moulded signature. This is one of the first perfume bottles which Lalique designed for Coty*

Above: '*Applique Seville PM*', *a very dramatic frosted glass chandelier, height 71 cm 28 in, which Lalique made circa 1920*

1925 Exposition des Arts Décoratifs established his reputation as a creative genius in the manufacture of decorative glassware. The new style, known as art deco, was now the trend in most art forms; the square and the rectangular was replacing the curved and the linear. Nevertheless most experts consider that Lalique never fully abandoned his art nouveau traditions, and although many of his glass creations are clearly in the art deco manner, a considerable number of his works are a mixture of the two.

Mass production

Lalique had a highly developed business sense, which contrasted strangely with his individualistic creative style. It was almost as though he wished to place his glass within the reach of all classes of society. Many of his works were produced in their thousands at his glass factory at Wingen sur Moder, which by the 1930s was employing a work force of over 600. Although during his later years René Lalique suffered from an arthritic condition which proved a serious handicap, this did not prevent him from maintaining his authority as the exclusive designer at his glass factory.

Towards the end of Lalique's life, production costs became an overwhelming factor in the manufacture of his glass. The designing and manufacture of large-style, one-off creations was no longer commercially viable, so the

d'Alsace René Lalique et Cie, built at Wingen sur Moder. It was here that some of the largest Lalique glass creations were made. Many of his pieces played a role in architecture; Lalique was one of the first to make a feature of decorated glass in doors, windows and lampshades, in houses, churches and hotels.

Lalique and art deco

Just as the Paris Exposition of 1900 established Lalique as a master craftsman of art nouveau jewellery, so the

Opposite: '*Paons*' *(Peacocks) lamp, 41.5 cm 16½ in. Circa 1908*

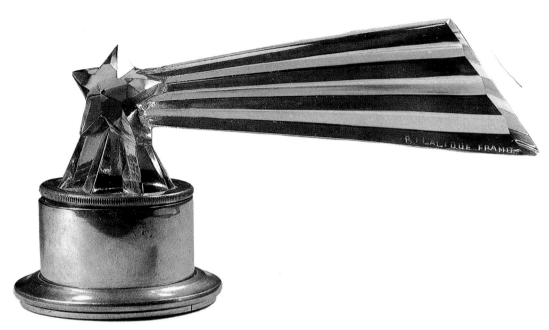

factory's production turned to press-moulded glass which was relatively inexpensive and carried little business risk. Some commissioned works were still executed, however, including some large glass pieces for use in churches and a few architectural pieces designed for department stores, hotels, trans-atlantic liners and for stands at international exhibitions.

The Combs la Ville glass works was shut in 1937, and the outbreak of World War II forced the Wingen sur Moder factory to close when it was occupied by the Germans. Shortly after the ending of hostilities in Europe, René Lalique died on 9 May 1945, at the age of eighty-five.

Post-war Lalique

The factory was reoccupied in late 1945, when René's son, Marc, undertook a massive programme of renovation and re-equipment. Marc Lalique introduced a new form of crystal glass which had a brighter and more translucent appearance than the pre-war metal. He designed many new glass products for the Wingen works and was joined by his daughter, Marie-Claude Lalique, in 1956. She carried on the family tradition of designing and producing fine decorative glass and took over the factory when her father died in 1977. The factory has always maintained the reputation established by René Lalique and today is still one of the leading glass manufacturers in the world.

Above: 'Comete', circa 1928. Height 19 cm $7\frac{1}{2}$ in. This clear glass car mascot is a very striking piece of geometric art deco design and personifies speed

Opposite: A covered vase in brilliant blue glass with a satin finish. There is a pattern of devil masks around the neck. Approx. 20 cm 8 in

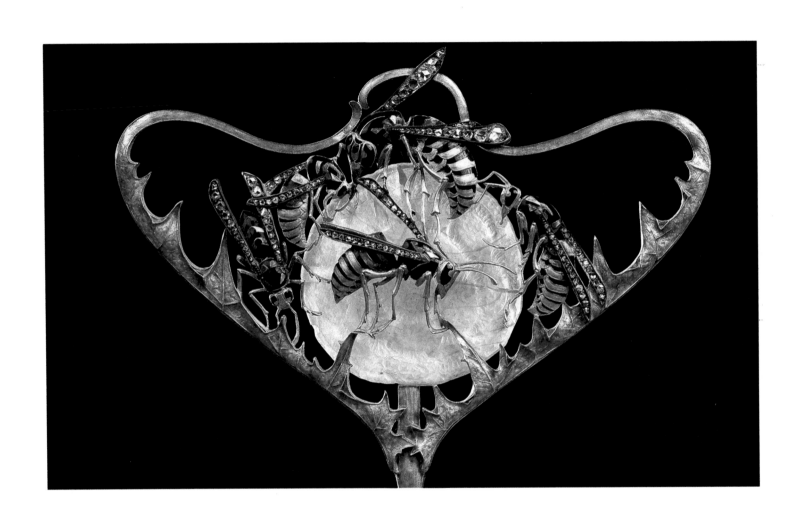

Wasps pin of gold, enamel, opal and diamonds. 1899–1900. Height 21 cm 8$\frac{1}{4}$ in

Chapter One

ART NOUVEAU JEWELRY

René Lalique has been described as the greatest artist-jeweller the world has ever known. Employing the fashionable motifs of the art nouveau period – a series of images from nature and the female form in writhing, sinuous movement – he created a series of pieces of astoundingly dramatic jewellery with erotic, decadent overtones. He was also a brilliant innovator, adding materials like horn, rock crystal and semiprecious stones to the traditional jeweller's repertoire and experimenting with many techniques, not previously used for jewellery. The result was a breathtaking range of pendants, brooches, necklaces, bracelets, hair ornaments and rings, unlike anything which had ever been seen before.

Although the main function of jewellery is to adorn and flatter the wearer, and it clearly belongs among the decorative arts, it has an economic and social function as well. The last decades of the 19th century were a period of tremendous upheaval and transformation, and this left its mark on the jewellery of that time.

Women were playing a more active role in daily life and were beginning to demand political emancipation and a more positive position in society. At the same time they rejected mid-19th century taste in fashion: elaborate, sombre dresses began to disappear; vulgar, mechanically made jewellery became unpopular, and there was no longer a demand for baroque and classical styles of jewellery.

The influence of Japan

As we have seen, the Japanese exhibitions which were being held in the capitals of the western world at this time acted as a catalyst in the decorative arts, including jewellery. Trade between Japan and the outside world had been non-existent for over 200 years until the restoration of the Meiji Emperors in the 1850s opened closed doors and permitted a new east–west trade to develop. Those who viewed the prints, ceramics, textiles and sculptures at the Japanese exhibitions were seeing art

Above: Diadem, circa 1902–03, with a pronounced Japanese influence. Two gold and enamel grasshoppers are poised, face to face, on a flowering branch. 8.4 cm 3½ in

forms which to them were entirely innovative and original in concept. A demand was immediately created for these exotic objects, which the jewellers of the day were quick to recognize and satisfy.

New materials

During the art nouveau period, there was still a vogue for valuable classical jewellery. Nothing could ever quite displace the pride of the wealthy in displaying magnificent diamonds and other precious stones mined in the furthest corners of the world. However, valuable stones became less important in jewellery design as interest increased in the use of unfamiliar substances to create something fresh and original. Semiprecious stones representing different colours in naturalistic forms became fashionable. Materials which could give an iridescent look to decorative items were sought after and used in all conceivable shapes and sizes.

Nowhere has fashion in women's adornment and dress been better understood than in France. Where French designers led, the rest of the world followed, no more so than in the new-found form of art nouveau jewellery design. The great French jewellers had always been masters in the techniques of the goldsmith and the silversmith. Craftsmen like Vever and Gaillard soon established themselves as creators of works in the naturalistic manner of art nouveau. In the forefront of this trend was René Lalique.

French art nouveau jewellery always expressed itself in the most original and

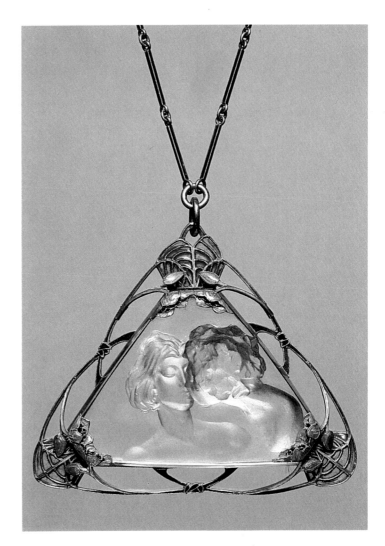

Above: *The kiss pendant, circa 1904–05. 4.7 cm 2 in. The figures are of rock crystal and the openwork surround is gold and green enamel with* plique à jour *at the corners*

pure style; it utterly rejected established traditional designs, especially those which had dominated the market until the 1850s and 1860s. New materials and new designs became the order of the day, with European jewel-

lers drawing exclusively on oriental art for their inspiration. However, René Lalique's early jewellery creations were produced to traditional designs which he succeeded in selling to the famous Parisian jewellery houses of Aucoc, Cartier and Boucheron. He also had close associations with Samuel Bing, a German who was a publisher and connoisseur of oriental art, as well as being a leading art dealer in Paris. Bing did much to gain international recognition for the art nouveau movement; he was highly enthusiastic about the aesthetic qualities of Japanese art and was responsible for importing many oriental works for sale in his shop, Maison de l'Art Nouveau, which became a meeting place for designers and avant-garde artists. These artefacts doubtless had an influence on Lalique's early designs.

Some of Lalique's innovatory jewellery creations were so dramatic that they were not always accepted as commercially viable. It is on record that in 1887 he designed a parure depicting a flight of swallows which the jeweller Boucheron dismissed as being 'too fantastic', and it was only after Lalique had implemented the design and Boucheron was able to see the magnificent result that the piece was immediately purchased. This parure led to the placing of many further commissions.

Left: Autumn pendant, circa 1898–1900. 9.5 cm 3¾ in. The pale female face, wreathed with gold plane leaves and enamelled branches and berries, represents the dying year

Above: *Japanese* netsuke. *On the left is a wasp on its nest (see page 28). 5 cm 2 in. On the right is a cicada perched on a leaf. 5.6 cm 2¼ in*

Lalique and traditional Japanese art forms

From the beginning, Lalique's jewellery pieces exhibited certain characteristics which showed that he had made detailed observations of Japanese artefacts, particularly in his study of *tsuba*, or sword guards. The trailing grapevine and trellis designs which were handworked on the metal guards and mounts of Japanese ceremonial swords were cleverly executed in 15 different metals interworked in contrasting colours. Other sword guards of the Japanese Edo period (1615–1868) were made in the form of a leaf. Two different metals were used to convey the effect of the varying shades of colour of the top and the underside of the leaf; even the veins were depicted, with insect holes contributing a realistic note – a typical feature adapted by art nouveau in its cut-out style of design.

Netsuke, small carved objects made as belt toggles and carved into every conceivable natural form, in masterpieces of miniature design, inspired Lalique, as

did the delicately carved *inro*, little tiered boxes for carrying seals, tobacco and other basic necessities of life, with their decoration of pine, bamboo and the ubiquitous Japanese chrysanthemum painted in gold lacquer. The Japanese *netsuke* makers did not hesitate to include rats, birds of prey, insects, snakes, frogs, toads, newts, lizards and snails in their work. A skull covered with maggots, a worm-eaten straw hat entwined with a trailing plant creeper, an octopus with closely entwined legs and frightening protruding eyes, and many similar examples symbolized the transience of life. Although some of the forms of Japanese *netsuke* are repugnant to European taste, those carved in the form of insects and reptiles do show marked similarities to some of Lalique's jewellery pieces.

In the British Museum there is a wooden *netsuke* of a wasp upon a nest, with cells containing minute larvae which are freely carved so that they move when the piece is shaken. René Lalique must have seen objects like these at the Japanese exhibitions, and at Samuel Bing's shop. He cannot have failed to be impressed and inspired, and he was not bound by the same restrictions as the Japanese craftsmen. As in Japan the *netsuke* was intended to be in constant functional use, the finished article needed to be smooth and articles carved in the form of insects and animals could not have protruding legs or arms which would break easily. Lalique was not inhibited in this way, and insect legs, wings and antennae feature frequently in his jewellery.

Novelty, vitality and invention were constantly sought by the carvers of

Above: Tsuba *(Japanese sword guard), 19th century, inlaid with gold, silver, copper and* sentoku, *showing Lao-tse, Buddha and Confucius drinking sake*

these exquisite *netsuke*, who, like Lalique, utilized all kinds of materials. Although most *netsuke* were fashioned in lacquer, wood and ivory, they were also made from metal, pottery, porcelain, tortoiseshell and horn. It should be remembered that the Japanese have always attempted the most complicated, challenging designs and methods of execution, for in the East art is appraised in accordance with its qualities of craftsmanship, whereas Western art is appreciated more in terms of its artistic effect. Lalique managed to attain the artistic ideals of both East and West. He enjoyed the challenge presented by unusual naturalistic forms that were sometimes grotesque and bizarre, taking the Japanese carvings and sculptures less popular in the West as his models.

A pendant and chain in the Lalique Museum in Japan has two beetles of green enamelled glass facing each other with their heads pressing against a centrally carved citrine. Their spindly legs are realistically carved in gold which has been enamelled dark green, and their segmented antennae are curved around their bodies to support an opal drop. This jewel, probably derived from Lalique's interest in Japanese metalwork, is typical of many of his insect creations.

As we have seen, many distinctive Japanese features are to be seen in the shape and colours of art nouveau jewellery, and the landscape jewellery, with its simple designs inspired by nature and the seasons, may be compared with the classic Japanese woodblock prints of landscapes. The art nouveau method of cut-out relief is very similar, too, to the Japanese practice in print-making of emphasizing certain characteristics by the use of a sharp silhouette.

Below: *'The Wave' by the Japanese painter, Hokusai (1760–1849). A leading member of the Ukiyo-ye (popular) school, his work influenced many Western artists*

Artists of René Lalique's stature could not fail to be influenced by these eastern ideas. Even while studying in England, Lalique must have been aware of the contribution that the Japanese were making to the metamorphosis of European and Western art, and its effects upon Morris's newly founded Arts and Crafts Movement. The Exposition Retrospective de l'Art Japonais, organized by Louis Gonse and Georges Petit in Paris in 1883, followed by the Exposition de la Gravure Japonaise in 1890 at L'Ecole des Beaux Arts and the many French publications written on the Japanese arts played a vital part in providing Lalique with basic ideas and a firm groundwork upon which he was able to expand and develop his own distinctive style.

Some of Lalique's insect and reptilian creations, as previously mentioned, did not always meet with the approval of the *bijoutiers*. Although his craftsmanship was always recognized for the superb artistry it undoubtedly was, the subject matter was at times too startling, frightening, even. Not all ladies of fashion wanted to wear the realistically carved, crawling insects, which were described by some contemporary critics as decadent, and the uncomfortable form and shape of some of Lalique's jewellery did not always sit happily next to a lady's skin. The edges were not always rounded and unfortunately the sharp metals sometimes proved impractical to wear. In fact it has been suggested that some of Lalique's more outstandingly naturalistic pieces were made to be worn by men. At the turn of the century homosexuals became socially acceptable in France, and as they required the very latest in fashion, ultra-modern jewellery was designed with them in mind.

Below: Brooch with dark brown patinated blister beetles on silver branches with enamel and glass berries. A tourmaline forms the centrepiece. Width 16 cm 6¼ in

Above: *Working drawing for the Winter woodland pendant (right). The pendant has a central panel of moulded intaglio glass with a gold enamelled frame. Circa 1899*

Overleaf (left): *Thistle bracelet, circa 1900–02, in silver, gold and dark blue enamel. 18.3 × 8 cm $7\frac{1}{4}$ × $3\frac{3}{4}$ in*

Overleaf (right): *Lalique's magnificent dragonfly corsage ornament, circa 1897–98, made of gold, enamel, chrysoprase, moonstones and diamonds. 27 × 26.5 cm $10\frac{3}{4}$ × $10\frac{1}{2}$ in*

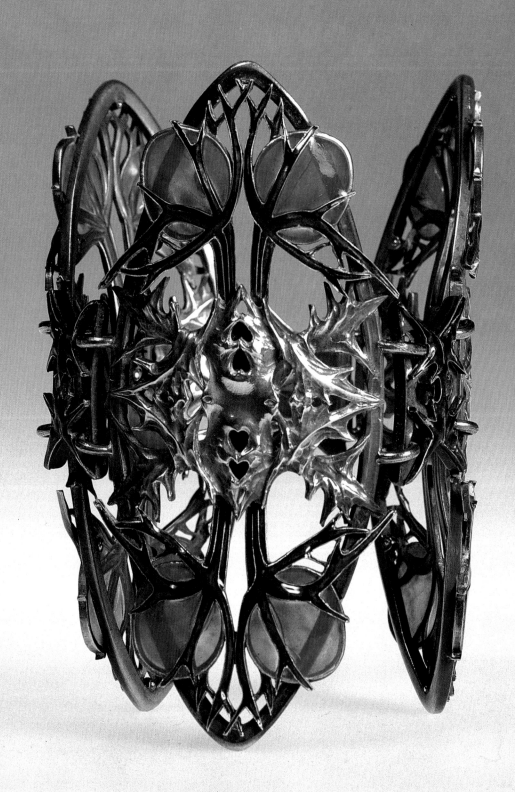

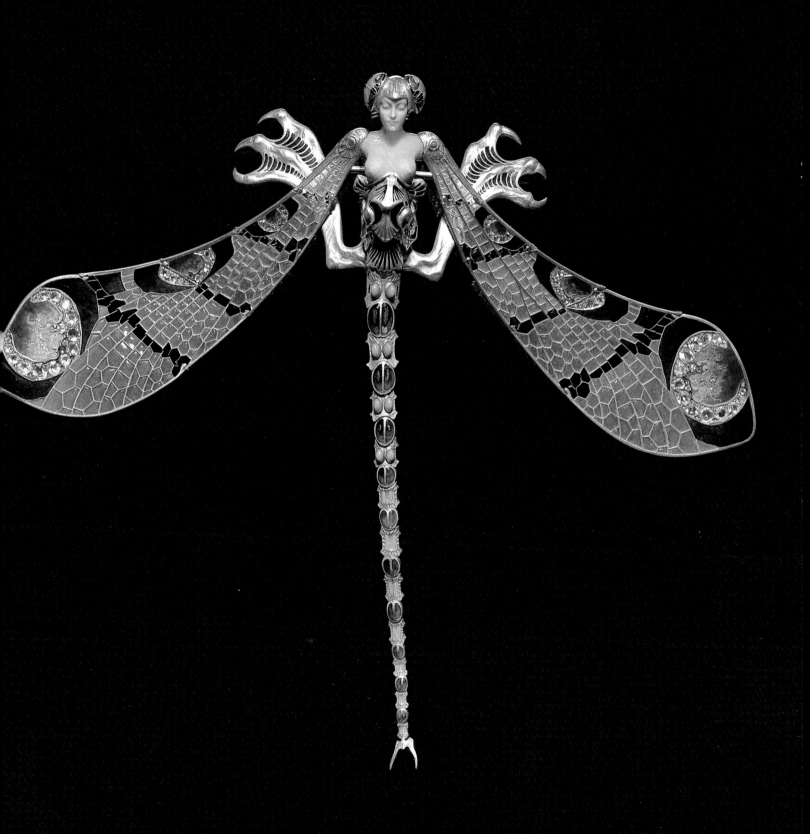

Lalique's financial success was established around 1892–4 when he was commissioned by Sarah Bernhardt to make an elaborate set of jewels to be worn in her role as Theodora. Sarah Bernhardt was intensely interested in the arts: indeed she was acknowledged as a sculptress herself, and was sufficiently accomplished to have some of her bronze works shown at the Exposition Universelle in Paris in 1900. She was a patron of a number of leading artists of the art nouveau school.

Parisian women of the belle époque, particularly courtesans of the demi-monde and women of the theatre, vied with each other in their efforts to attract the attentions of young French intellectuals, and the more bizarre and outrageous their articles of adornment

Above: *A landscape dog collar plaque, circa 1900, in the* plique à jour *technique, featuring Lalique's pine cone motif*

the better. Such tastes were catered for admirably by the new school of art nouveau jewellers, who created extraordinary pieces with themes which have often been described as decadent and demented. Sinuous, sensual and attenuated forms expressing erotic overtones, sexual immorality and danger and inspiring feelings of revulsion were all characteristic of these artistic creations. The writhing snake, traditionally associated with evil, though also a symbol of wisdom, was a favourite motif. Indeed, the snake has been popular in jewellery from ancient

Greek and Roman times, its long, sinuous form and brilliant colours providing an ideal subject. A magnificent gold bracelet and a ring in the form of a coiled snake, heavily inlaid with opals, emeralds and diamonds, the head of aquamarine enamels with ruby eyes, was made for Sarah Bernhardt by the Paris jeweller Georges Fouquet after a drawing by Alphonse Mucha.

It is thought that Mucha was responsible for introducing Lalique to Sarah Bernhardt. The jewels Lalique made for her were of large, theatrical proportions and were enthusiastically received by her spellbound audiences. Commissions for other work quickly followed: in fact it is probable that Sarah Bernhardt was able to gain some commissions on his behalf during her world tour in 1892. Certainly after her visit to St Petersburg and Moscow in 1896 a landscape brooch featuring 'Winter', exhibited at the Paris Salon, was ordered by a Russian.

These landscape brooches are particularly beautiful and are such fine examples of the craftsman's skill that the enamels seem almost to have been applied with a paint-brush. The method employed, termed *plique à jour*, is very similar to the oriental art of *cloisonné* work, which has been practised by the Chinese since the early days of the Ming Dynasty, although its origins date back even further: Persian and Byzantine examples of inlaid enamel work on metal were probably introduced into China by the Mongolian invaders.

The term *cloisonné* literally means 'inlaid between partitions or fences'; the design is outlined with bent wires forming fillets or strips (*cloisons*). Usually of brass, silver, copper or gold, the *cloisons* are placed upon a metal base, to which they are soldered. The various stages in *cloisonné* work are quite lengthy and complex, as the design has first to be drawn upon the metal ground before the *cloisons* are filled in with the coloured enamels and then fired. There may be several firings depending on the complexity of the design.

This exacting craftsmanship presented no problem to the Japanese who have always been exceptionally talented in metal decoration, and outshone even the Chinese, producing the most complicated and complex patterns which they considered a challenge to their expertise. The first Japanese enamels were made in the early 17th century, but it was not until the 1867 Paris Exposition that the artistic merits of Japanese *cloisonné* were fully appreciated by Westerners. Japan is also noted for producing *cloisonné* enamels upon a porcelain base, a small step away from *plique à jour*, in which the ground is removed, usually by acid, and the enamels held in suspension between the *cloisons*. The Japanese have practised this type of metalwork, which they call *shotai jippo* (removal of metal base and/or *cloisons*) since the 18th century. The method lends itself ideally to jewellery, particularly art nouveau jewellery with its portrayals of flying insects such as beetles, bees, wasps, dragonflies and butterflies, with their transparent, iridescent wings, or to depict leaves with threadlike veins, so often the central theme of Lalique's jewellery.

Most of Lalique's *cloisons* were made of gold, a metal unsurpassed in its versatility. For example, it can be hammered into the thinnest gold leaf and is so ductile that it can even be spun into gold thread. Gold also reflected perfectly the varying colours of the enamels which Lalique used to such brilliant effect.

Another style of workmanship practised by Lalique which was also in evidence in much Japanese metalwork, was the art of *champlevé*, in which the surface of the metal is chiselled out or engraved so that the enamels can be laid into the depressions. The base of objects to be finished in a *champlevé* design was usually cast in bronze, but because of the difficulty of carving bronze the designs were necessarily much more simple than in *cloisonné* work.

It was not uncommon to find both *cloisonné* and *champlevé* combined in the same piece of jewellery, depending on the nature of the design. There is hardly any material with which Lalique did not at some time experiment. The shape and colour of the finished piece were always his prime consideration, rather than the use of the more expensive and more generally accepted jeweller's stock-in-trade of gold, silver, diamonds and other precious stones. If he could achieve the desired result using the humblest of materials, so much the better. As well as semiprecious stones, he was particularly interested in the properties of enamels with their varying characteristics of opaqueness, opalescence, transparency and translucency. He also experimented with organic materials – horn, tortoiseshell, ivory and leather.

Fashion accessories

Ladies of fashion in the late Victorian and Edwardian periods, as well as having rigidly corseted, hour-glass figures, were required to have mountains of hair piled high to support vast picture hats. These hats were placed carefully in a horizontal position to act as large trays laden with ostrich feathers, fur, birds, flowers, and fruit and were secured to the elaborate coiffure beneath with very long hatpins. Some of these were almost 25 cm (10 inches) in length and they became important fashion accessories, made to intricate designs and ornamented with precious stones. One such hatpin was shown at the 1987 Goldsmiths' Company Exhibition in London, which featured over 200 of Lalique's outstanding jewellery creations. Previously exhibited at the Exposition Universelle in Paris in 1900 and purchased by the Danish Museum of Decorative Art in Copenhagen, the pin is an outstanding example of the originality of Lalique's artistic genius. Over 20 cm (8 inches) long, it is made from gold enamel, opal and diamonds. The central focal point is an opal, carved to represent a flower-head which gives the

Opposite: Working drawing for Eagles and pine trees dog collar plaque (top). The plaque (below), is of openwork gold and enamel with an opal. H. 5.5 cm 2¼ in

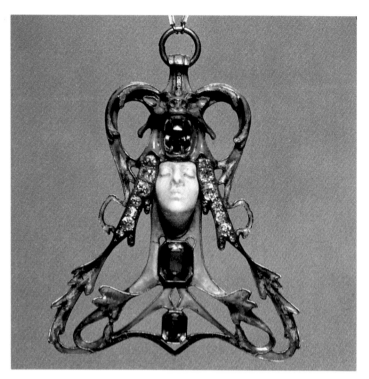

Above, left: *Wild beast pendant of gold, ivory, enamel, diamonds and sapphires,*
Right: *Pendant/brooch, gold, enamel, diamonds, quartz, glass. Both c.1900*

impression of a honey-pot, supporting five wasps with striped bodies made of gold and enamels, their wings glinting with diamonds. The eyes and feet of each wasp are delicately carved to reveal the detailed appendages and joints. The whole is contained within a gold and blue enamelled triangular outline of simulated foliage with heavily veined and pointed fern-like leaves, which somehow convey a sense of decadence and decay. The pin creates an image of greed and death, yet one cannot but admire the intricate and realistic artistry with which Lalique has succeeded in capturing the very essence of nature. The wasps are modelled so realistically that they almost appear to be alive and moving.

Many other functional items for use in dressing hair were made in the Lalique workshop. Combs and hair ornaments were skilfully carved in organic materials. Punched leather inset with semiprecious stones and glass was used on bracelets, collars and pectorals. Lalique was also able to achieve the most unusual shapes in carved horn by experimenting with heating it, to make it more malleable. In fact Lalique was the first to adapt the art of sculpting horn for use in jewellery. He recognized the versatility of this organic substance and the translucent effects which could be achieved by carving it to varying thicknesses. He made a large number of horn haircombs, some of which were also exhibited at the Goldsmiths' Hall. They represented varying plant forms carved to almost paper-like thinness which permitted light to filter through and project an impression of sunlight. Sometimes the overall effect was enhanced by the presence of small patinated insects carved from semiprecious stones, crawling over the flower and foliage heads. These are stunning examples of Lalique's innovatory talent in turning a simple functional object into something breathtakingly beautiful.

Lalique also carved and shaped horn with superb effect to create tiaras, which at that time were an integral part of the toilette of the fashionable elite. In striking contrast with the classical diamond tiaras of Cartier, Lalique made his tiaras resemble forbidding-looking bats' wings studded with birch leaves and other plant forms: catkins, mimosa and plum blossom were represented by studded diamonds.

A horn necklace in the Calouste Gulbenkian Museum in Lisbon consists of pairs of grasshoppers, graduated in size, head to head, holding two baroque pearls between their front and hind feet. The horn is carved so thinly that in some places it looks like the wings of a bat in flight. This necklace is strangely sombre and dark, with some disquieting features. The influence of Japanese metalwork may be discerned in Lalique's craftsmanship. He skilfully used the varying colours of semiprecious stones such as cornelians, bloodstones, chrysoprase, onyx, jasper,

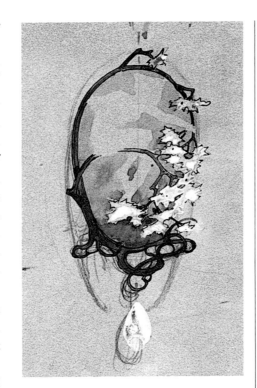

Above: *Working drawing for the Ivy nymph pendant. 28 × 22 cm 11 × 8½ in. Lalique's notes specified diamonds, but they were not included in the finished work*

chrysoberyls, citrines, chalcedony and demontoids, along with diamonds, rubies, pearls and opals, to contrast vividly with the surrounding metals and enamels. Almost every type of known stone was ingeniously portrayed to advantage in Lalique's creations.

Experiments with glass

It was during his jewellery-making period that René Lalique began to recognize the possibilities offered by the varying techniques of glass manufacture. His early experiments were made using powdered glass which was fired in

Above: *Grasshopper necklace, circa 1903, of carved and stained horn with baroque pearls. 19.5 × 56.5 cm 7¼ × 38¼ in*

a mould and then lightly enamelled, a process known as *pâte de verre*. These experiments were to be brought to full fruition in his later career when he became even more internationally famous for his outstanding contribution to glass-making than for his creative artistry as a designer of exotic art nouveau jewellery.

At first he used clear and coloured glass as a medium which he sometimes engraved with plants, female faces and landscape forms. He soon realized that sculpted glass gave an excellent three-dimensional effect to his jewellery pieces, which inspired him to use glass increasingly in this context. In the late 1890s Lalique made many small decorative objects using glass in conjunction with other materials, such as bronze, silver, ivory, foiled copper and alabaster.

Sculpture, too, always figured very prominently in Lalique's work. He used silver and gold in the making of medals, medallions and plaques; another of his favourite materials in this medium was bronze which he used to sculpt shallow relief medallions, usually featuring a woman's head. These were made as commemorative pieces for his exhibitions and bore striking resemblances to Roman and Greek medals and plaques. It has been suggested that their working was strongly influenced by Lalique's father-in-law, Auguste Ledru.

Tour à réduire

Lalique was the first jeweller to adopt the use of the *tour à réduire* method of reducing a life-sized profile to medallion size. This involved the use of a machine to scale down the relief carving of a large model to a much smaller area without loss of any detail. The method had been employed by medallists and coin-makers, but Lalique was the first person to use it in the making of jewellery. In the beginning he used *tour à réduire* to scale down ivory, but it was not long before he was also scaling down detailed casts in metal.

In 1896 he made a silver medal bearing a portrait of Sarah Bernhardt to commemorate one of her special matinée performances at the Théâtre de la Renaissance. It formed the frontispiece of the programme, and some of the medals were personally dedicated in ink on their reverse side by the actress and given to a few favoured guests.

Above: *Lalique's great patron, Calouste Sarkis Gulbenkian (1869–1955)*

Calouste Gulbenkian

Among Sarah Bernhardt's many admirers was the great arts patron Calouste Gulbenkian, known in the commercial world as 'Mister Five Per Cent', for his business acumen in acquiring a life-time interest in the petroleum output of Iraq. He became one of René Lalique's most rewarding patrons and around 1895 commissioned many items of jewellery from him. Gulbenkian owned a splendid mansion in Paris on the Avenue d'Iéna, which housed his extraordinarily fine art collection, including old master paintings,

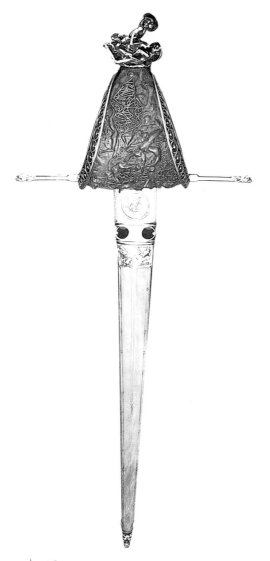

Above: *Dagger, circa 1900, 60.5 cm 24 in. The hilt, of carved horn in a silver setting, shows a battle scene in high relief. The finial is two fighting silver figures*

numbered over 150 and were representative of Lalique's entire range. Lalique was given a free hand to create whatever he desired, in any shape, colour or material – a creative artist's dream. The resulting pieces of jewellery were never meant to be worn, but to illustrate the full range of Lalique's creative imagination. Fantasy reigned supreme and covered almost every aspect of the animal, insect and marine world.

When Lalique showed his work at Agnew's in 1905, as well as showcases of brooches, rings, earrings, bracelets, necklaces, collars embroidered in gold and silver thread, pendants, tiaras, diadems, combs, hair ornaments, hatpins, buckles, clasps and stomachers, there were other superb examples of his sculptural skills: statuettes, seals, watches, goblets, silver clasps, purses, salt and pepper mills, silver table pieces, horn knives, silver enamelled cups and saucers, inkwells, daggers of rhinoceros horn and gold boxes encrusted with opals and semiprecious stones. Some of these boxes were decorated in high relief, with swirls and arabesques ending in flower-tipped tendrils, all with the slight asymmetry that typifies art nouveau. Some were framed in a pattern of lianas which appeared to be hideously alive.

A focal point of Agnew's exhibition was a large silver centrepiece, over 60 cm (24 inches) in height, set on an oval base measuring approximately 60 cm × 100 cm (24 inches × 42 inches). It used to stand on a centre table in Lalique's Paris showrooms at Cours la Reine until Gulbenkian acquired it.

fine sculptures and porcelain. Many fine cabinets were specially constructed to house René Lalique's jewellery and *objets de vertu* purchased from Lalique's earlier exhibitions in London and Paris. These series of commissioned objects

Above: *The silver centrepiece which created a sensation when it was exhibited at Agnew's*
London gallery in 1905

The central motif is of a naked naiad or water nymph draped in seaweed and standing upon a water lily, and the piece is sculpted in silver upon a glass base in imitation of a pond. There are four other silver nymphs around the rim, all holding fish, from whose open mouths cascades moulded glass in imitation of gushing water. It is an *objet de vertu* of extraordinary proportions in the art nouveau taste.

Sometimes the asymmetrical design of an object is dictated by the use of semiprecious stones cut in cabochon shapes, the reflective surfaces creating flashing colours. Although Lalique did not entirely reject the use of precious stones, he did prefer gem stones of rare and unusual shapes and colours. An example of this preference may be illustrated by his frequent use of the baroque pearl. He did not favour a perfect circular or pear shape: instead, he would use the sometimes grotesque outline of a misshapen pearl in an enamelled setting to create a mysterious, enigmatic effect. A pendant acquired by Gulbenkian in 1901, called the 'Poppy Maiden', is composed of a cast glass face overlaid with opalescent enamel and surrounded by swirling hair made from oxidized silver. The head is crowned with open poppies and the features have a trance-like expression, conveying a suggestion of opium addiction, perhaps confirmed by the presence of poppies in the design. A hanging baroque pearl is supported by tresses of hair. This jewel has a languorous, dreamlike quality which exudes an atmosphere of brooding mystery.

Above: Poppy maiden pendant, circa 1898–1900. The cast glass face overlaid with opalescent enamel and its garland of silver poppies, symbolizes sleep. 7 cm 2¾ in

Insects and flowers

Many of Lalique's jewellery pieces, especially those featuring sculpted insects, convey a sense of unease. A corsage ornament acquired by Gulbenkian in 1904 and now in the Calouste Gulbenkian Collection in Lisbon, features two dark brown blister beetles made from shining patinated silver. They are facing each other with outstretched pincers and appear to be fighting over a large red tourmaline. The centre of the ornament is not unlike dripping blood, while the overall effect is of some evil medieval instrument of torture.

These extraordinary effects are confirmed when one examines in depth other masterpieces by Lalique. As we have seen, he sometimes took his inspiration from the Japanese *netsuke* carvers by making his insects actually move: the wings of a dragonfly are made to fold and close; appendages are hinged and jointed and move freely. He even manages to create a disconcerting effect by his decoration of insect wings. While the colours are always quite beautiful and realistic, he sometimes places dark coloured stones upon a wing, which adds an ominous, disturbing note by giving the insect extra 'eyes'.

Many of the more bizarre sculptures employ a skeletal theme, using the veins of wings to produce a magnetic effect to which the eye is automatically attracted. Lalique employed this extremely original idea when he designed the group of five bronzes which formed a focal point for his stand at the Exposition Universelle in Paris in 1900.

Above: *'Anemones flétries' (Fading anemones), a pendant of gold, enamel and frosted glass on an enamelled foliate chain. The anemones are made of pale lavender glass. Circa 1905. 6.6 cm 2½ in*

They formed a decorative grille, each patinated bronze taking the shape of a winged female nude with flowers in her hair, and her hands clasped under her chin. The extended wings were not unlike those of a giant swallowtail butterfly and formed the main part of the grille, which stood about 100 cm (42 inches) high. The backs of the bronzed skeletal wings were draped with clear gauze upon which Lalique pinned some of his pieces of jewellery. The overall

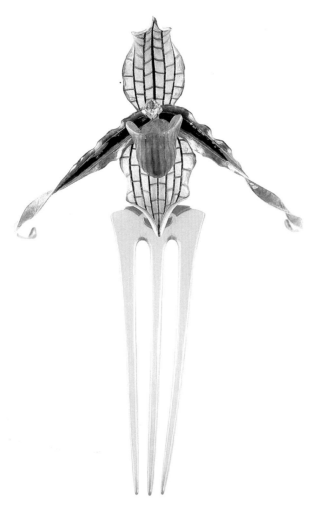

Above: Orchid hair comb, circa 1902, of gold, glass, horn and enamel. The erotic overtones of the orchid made it a favourite motif of art nouveau artists

The flowers of the art nouveau jewellers were very much more lifelike; and they were often modelled in bud. Many of Lalique's flowers, too, are not in full bloom, although, like many of the art nouveau designers, he also employed the swirling lines of full-blown lilies, irises, anemones and other popular flowers of the period.

He often used orchid blooms with dramatic effect. This exotic hot-house plant with its overtones of sexuality was a favourite motif of the artists working in the art nouveau manner. Its brightly coloured petals and sepals conveying an air of richness provided an excellent vehicle for the use of brightly coloured enamels and semiprecious stones. A three-pronged horn comb mounted with a cypripedium orchid, in the Anderson Collection at the Sainsbury Centre for Visual Arts, University of East Anglia, Norwich, is a typical example of Lalique's favourite use of the orchid design. The petals are formed of yellow and brown enamels, with the name 'Lalique' stamped on one of them. The centre of this exotic flower is formed in cast glass with a cut diamond of trapezium shape. The scale is characteristically large and the comb measures no less than 19 cm (7½ inches) in height.

A gold and enamel buckle from the same collection is quite breathtaking in its beauty. It is designed as two stylized butterflies joined, by hinges, on either side of a central opal cabochon. The wings of each butterfly are richly coloured in shades of blue *plique à jour* enamelling. The top edge of each wing

effect was startling, with erotic overtones, and added to the general air of excitement at this exhibition of *fin-de-siècle* art.

Much of the jewellery before art nouveau featured diamonds and rubies to represent flowers in full bloom, but despite all the efforts of the jewellers these pieces appeared stiff and lifeless.

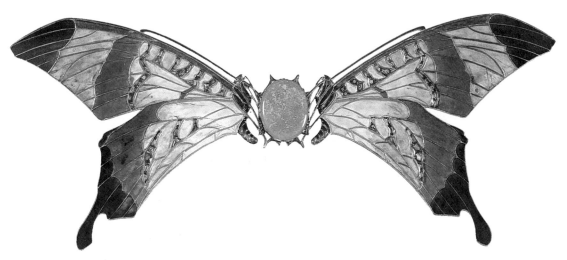

Above: Butterflies buckle, circa 1903–4
7.2 × 18.2 cm 3 × 7½ in. This piece
features two gold and enamel swallowtail
butterflies clasping an opal beetle

bears the mark 'Lalique' stamped on the
gold metal. In fact it has sometimes
been thought that the buckle comprises
a single butterfly because of the exact
symmetry of the insects with their
folded wings facing each other. This
buckle is over 19 cm (7½ inches) wide
and 7½ cm (3 inches) high.

Many of Lalique's more extravagant
masterpieces displayed the human
female head and body in conjunction
with other animal forms. An example of
this type of jewellery in the Calouste
Gulbenkian Collection is a very large
dragonfly corsage ornament over
25 × 25 cm (10 × 10 inches) portraying
a nightmarish image with macabre
overtones. The ornament comprises an
articulated dragonfly body of gold, decorated with chrysoprase cabochons
and dark blue enamels. The wings have
plique à jour enamelling in iridescent
shades of blue-green, with markings of
pooled moonstones and diamonds.
However, it is the dragonfly's head
which immediately attracts the attention, for from its jaws emerges the full-
breasted figure of a woman, carved in
chrysoprase. She is wearing a gold hel-
met enamelled with two scarabs and her
arms metamorphose into the insect's
wings. To further emphasize the mor-
bidity and sense of revulsion created by
this piece, two huge predatory claws
made of gold and enamel extend from
either side of the dragonfly's body, as if
ready to maim its prey. The savage
beauty of this jewel, also in the Calouste
Gulbenkian Collection, never fails to
arouse comment: more than any other
piece of Lalique jewellery, it symbolizes a new beginning and a new age, the
birth of a new century.

Another example of the female form
metamorphosing, together with the
image of arms developing into wings, is
provided by the particularly fine and
beautifully proportioned so-called
Swan Necklace, belonging to the Lillian
Nassau Collection which is in the Metro-

politan Museum of Art in New York. It comprises nine gold female nudes, each in an elongated, statuesque pose, their arms extending outwards and downwards in a winged or cloaked effect, worked in green *plique à jour* enamels and enclosing the whole body. At the feet of each figure is a pair of purple, black and gold swans pecking at golden reeds which surround an oval cabochon amethyst. Between each female motif are large opals encased in swirling leaves of gold hanging from another cabochon amethyst contained within the necklet. The feature which makes this piece so startling is undoubtedly the figures' hair. This is composed of black enamelling set within gold *champlevé* work, made to represent eight separate locks, two of which are akin to the horns of a stag beetle. In fact the figures have been taken to represent nine primeval insects, and have also been likened to Medusa's head.

Lalique was well acquainted with the actresses and dancers of the belle époque in *fin-de-siècle* Paris and proved himself more than capable of satisfying their desire for jewels with macabre, sensual overtones. When cost was immaterial he allowed his creative imagination to run free, extending his eclectic talents to the full and catering for all tastes. His female nudes represent unbridled sensuality and many of his animal and plant forms contain a blend of sexuality and death.

The 1900 Paris Exposition proved the triumphal apex of Lalique's jewellery career, and thereafter museums all over the world vied with each other to acquire some of the master's work. Lalique was acclaimed as the undisputed leading jeweller of the age, and was flooded with orders from the major cities of Germany, Denmark, Italy, Austria, England and the United States of America. Exhibitions were held in Turin in 1902, Berlin in 1903 and St Louis in 1904.

New directions

As the 20th century began, some of Lalique's jewels began to adopt the new art deco style. They took on a new geometricity, square and rectangle forms making an appearance on some of his brooches and pins. He started to experiment with the use of steel and aluminium in his jewel settings, cutting and etching them sharply to give a polished, shining effect, not unlike the new art forms introduced by the German designers at the 1910 Paris Exposition.

The delicate tendrils and curves of art nouveau began to go out of fashion and styles became more formalized and materials more basic with the discovery and introduction of bakelite, for example. As Lalique's mastery of deliquescence and the superb artistry he employed in the sculpting of gold and other precious metals to give a suggestion of growth, energy and vitality became less popular, he began to experiment increasingly with glass.

Around 1906 he designed a corsage ornament which illustrated the new levels of artistry he was achieving in his use of this medium. This piece of jewellery, designed in a simpler, more

classical style, is known as the Doves of Peace. It has a central motif of two plump doves sculpted in frosted crystal glass, perched on an olive branch with thick clusters of diamond leaves in a gold setting. There are two groups of three other doves on either side of this pair, sculpted within the olive branches. The doves are modelled so realistically that the varying shades of their plumage can be seen. Their feet are enamelled in black on gold and the whole supported a diamond drop. The

Above: Swan necklace, of gold, opals and amethysts, circa 1900. Diameter 23.5 cm $9\frac{1}{2}$ in. This is one of the most dramatic of Lalique's pieces of art nouveau jewellery

corsage was adjudged a fitting gift for Mrs Edith Wilson, wife of the United States President, Woodrow Wilson, when he visited Europe for the Peace Conference in 1919. The President was given a Lalique box with frosted glass panels moulded with butterflies.

'Bouchon cassis', a rare scent bottle with a tiara stopper

Chapter Two

FIRST VENTURES INTO GLASS

Towards the close of the 19th century René Lalique began his first tentative experiments with glass. Some years later, partly as a reaction against the cheap imitations of his jewellery which were flooding the market, he turned his attention entirely to this new medium. 1907 marked the watershed – it was the year the Corsican entrepreneur, François Coty, commissioned first, labels and stoppers for his perfume bottles, and then the bottles themselves. In 1910 Lalique purchased a glassworks at Combs-la-Ville, near Paris, and his output of superbly crafted, mass-produced perfume bottles, *garnitures de toilette*, desk accessories, tableware and, of course, the dazzling range of vases, began in earnest.

misty, bisque result. These moulds were made of a refractory-fired clay or metal capable of withstanding the high temperature involved.

Objets de vertu

Initially Lalique did not use the purer form of lead crystal glass, but employed a demi-crystal which he considered to be more malleable. Instead of relying on the brightness of colours in the glass, he preferred to work with a clear, colourless substance. His early experiments resulted in small *objets de vertu* made of glass and metal. Each was designed and crafted individually and as such was unique. Vases and containers made from metal armatures shaped in art nouveau fashion, containing blown opalescent glass, were typical examples. Using glass in combination with other materials, Lalique conducted his own experiments in applying various temperatures to alabaster, copper, ivory, silver and bronze. His unique experience as a jeweller proved invaluable in fulfilling the demand for these small *objets de vertu* by his distinguished and now vast clientele.

His skill in sculpting bronzeware was evidenced by his production of glass plaques with a moulded intaglio decoration in bas relief featuring a wide variety of ornamentation, largely based on plant forms or female faces and figures. He also produced small glass statuettes of the female form in striking poses, which he sold in increasing numbers from his Paris shop. However, it was not until he moved to Clairefontaine near Rambouillet, where he

All Lalique's early experiments with glass took place at his small factory in the rue Thérèse, where he lived with his wife in a flat above the workshops on the ground floor. Most of the small pieces which he sculpted and crafted for use in his jewellery creations were made by the *pâte de verre* process. A mould was filled with pastel-coloured ground powdered glass which was subsequently fused by heating to give a

Above: *A cire perdue* frosted and stained vase mounted with a design of beech leaves. The name R. Lalique is just above the base. 15.8 cm 6.2 in

Opposite: *A chalice in opalescent glass overlaid with a silver mount with the pine cone motif, also found on the doors of Lalique's Paris atelier. Circa 1904. 20 cm 8 in*

rented a small factory and employed a select staff of four, that he began to develop his true skills in glass manufacture.

Cire Perdue

Lalique was the first to utilize glass in a decorative manner for architectural purposes and it was at Clairefontaine that he made his famous 'pine cone' doors for the front of his premises on the Cours la Reine in Paris. Shortly after commencing work at Clairefontaine, Lalique began to employ the *cire perdue* (lost wax) process to produce detailed sculpted work. This entailed the modelling in high relief of a figure, plant or animal form (sometimes laid into a vase or container shape) in wax. A mould was cast around the wax, leaving a small hole, the wax was then heated and poured away and, when it had cooled, molten glass poured into the mould. When the glass had cooled, the mould was carefully broken and a solid glass sculpture revealed.

Sometimes Lalique employed the *cire perdue* method of decoration on his *objets de vertu*. A chalice exhibited at Agnew's gallery, Bond Street, in London in 1905 and now in the Calouste Gulbenkian Collection in Lisbon, is made from a copper armature featuring a grape vine with trailing art nouveau decoration. The cup and foot are made from clear blown glass, while around the stem are several figures moulded by the *cire perdue* process. This outstandingly impressive object bears witness to the discerning artistic taste of Calouste Gulbenkian.

François Coty

Shortly after Lalique's move to Claire-fontaine, an event took place which was to have a profound effect upon the course of his future career. A new retail establishment, the House of Coty, opened near his Paris shop on the Place Vendôme in 1906. François Coty was a true entrepreneur of the 20th century. A native of Corsica, he arrived in Paris in 1900 with little capital but a great deal of business flair. He quickly noticed that the marketing of perfume and eau de cologne was very rudimentary, offering plenty of scope for improvement. At that time most perfume preparations were dispensed by chemists and sold in plain pharmaceutical bottles without any wrapper, label or brand name. Then a revolutionary change in

perfume production took place. Hitherto only natural materials of animal and vegetable origin had been employed in the manufacture of perfumes, making them extremely expensive, and in fact only the very wealthy could afford them. Then came the discovery by chemists of synthetic ingredients which, when correctly blended, gave almost the same aroma as natural products. Thanks to these synthetic substitutes, manufacturers were able to produce large quantities of good quality perfume at a reasonable price.

'La Rose Jacqueminot'

François Coty spent two years learning about the intricacies of blending aromatics at Grasse, the perfume centre in Provence. In 1905 he returned to Paris and borrowed money to launch his own perfume, 'La Rose Jacqueminot'. There is an amusing anecdote concerning this young man's salesmanship. Unable to convince one large retailer that he should place an order, despite the perfume's attractive name and smart bottle, Coty dropped the bottle on the floor, shattering it, and thus managed to attract the instant attention of several hundred potential customers. It did not take long for 'La Rose Jacqueminot' to become such a commercial success that it established Coty's name as a market leader for the next twenty years.

Left: *François Coty. A photograph of the great* parfumeur*, taken in the early years of his association with René Lalique*

Coty often visited the neighbouring shop owned by Lalique on the Place Vendôme where he admired the jewellery and *objets de vertu*. Sometimes Lalique included small decorative flasks and bottles among the various articles on display in his shop. These must have impressed Coty, for in 1907 he asked Lalique to design some labels for his perfume bottles, and it was not long before Lalique was designing the bottles as well.

At first Lalique did not have the facilities for large-scale bottle production and he designed only the decorative stoppers and labels, leaving the body of the bottles relatively plain and rectangular in form. These were made by Auguste J. F. Legras who had established a large glass factory at Saint Denis just outside Paris. These plain-bodied bottles do not bear a Lalique mark but they do sometimes display the name of Coty. The early bottles were not individually designed to contain different perfumes but could be used interchangeably, the contents being denoted by Lalique's gold labels.

The distinguishing feature which clearly indicates that these perfume bottles originated with Lalique may be discerned in the design and construction of their stoppers. Whereas the body of the early Coty perfume bottle is of clear, crisply moulded glass, typical of the Legras factory, the stoppers are individually cast in moulds of two sections to form a solid piece. Sometimes they have a frosted appearance with a sculpted art nouveau carving designed by the master's hand.

Above: *'Au Coeur des Calices', a scent bottle made for François Coty, before the First World War. 7 cm 2¾ in*

Lalique produced some special de luxe bottles for Coty, which were usually larger and made for wealthy clients. They were designed as a permanent feature of a lady's dressing table, to be refilled when empty. These examples of Lalique's early glass are now particularly sought after as collectors' items.

It was not long before the commercial success of Coty's perfumes swept across France, which became firmly established as the leader in the world perfume market – an achievement due in no small part to the artistry and creativity of Lalique. François Coty had the foresight to detect the chance of capturing a world market and he had the

noted for the local sand which was particularly suitable for glass making because of its high silicon content. He studied the mass production of glass in both the pharmaceutical and wine-making industries and very soon, with a staff of just under a hundred workers, he began to produce perfume bottles on a commercial scale for many of the major perfumeries. Lalique employed the very latest technology which he had studied at other glassworks, using precision-cast metal moulds to produce his decorative glassware. His commercial success was almost immediate and in 1910 he was able to buy the Combs La Ville glassworks.

Specially commissioned designs for perfume bottles were made for the firms of Roger et Gallet and D'Orsay as well as Coty. Some of these had stoppers designed in the shape of tiaras, or moulded and etched in the form of an inverted crescent moon as large as the bottle itself. Some bore extravagant designs of female nude figures draped amongst flowering vines or branches, while others were moulded in the shape of a flowering tree, with the trunk disappearing into the bottle. Occasion-

good fortune – and good sense – to obtain the services of René Lalique in furthering his aims. As society became increasingly affluent, so the demand for luxury items grew. The age of packaging had arrived and the perfume industry soon realized that a decorative bottle was as important a marketing feature as its contents.

The beginnings of a mass market

It was not long before Lalique began to capitalize upon his new venture into glass making. In 1909 he rented a glassworks at Combs La Ville, an area

Above left: *'Myosotis' flacon, part of a garniture de toilette. A kneeling nude, garlanded with flowers, forms the stopper. Circa 1920. 26 cm 10¼ in*

Opposite: *A selection of Lalique's perfume bottles. The large blue one and the clear ones with rings were made for Worth, one of Lalique's main parfumeur clients*

ally Lalique employed coloured glass for these stoppers (see 'Bouchon cassis' on page 50); these are extremely rare and very collectable.

It was not long before all the leading French perfumers were customers of Lalique: Houbigant, Forvil, Molinard, Arys, Guerlain, Morabito, Corday, Rigaud and Vigny. Some had their company names inscribed on the bottle, while others occasionally bore the inscribed brand name of the perfume. Each was a unique example of Lalique's artistry. While many of his early scent bottles were of clear undecorated glass, he soon employed a form of enamel to colour certain recessed areas in the glass decoration, a process called 'patine'. Many of Lalique's small perfume bottles were made as articles for functional use, yet they are recognized as works of art in their own right. The minute carving is quite exceptional: the

Below: *A scent bottle in clear and satin-finished glass, moulded in the shape of a cicada and engraved R. Lalique on one wing. 6.5 cm 2½ in long*

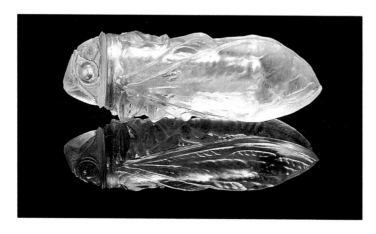

bottles were sculpted with an extraordinary variety of designs — flowers such as dahlias and forget-me-nots, female nude dancers and dancing couples in classical Greek dress, embossed mermaids, classical frieze designs patinated into varying shades of colour. Many bottles had frosted glass stoppers depicting beautifully carved female nudes, sometimes sensual nymphs kneeling holding their long tresses of hair. The art nouveau curvilinear form is evident in many of these early scent bottles.

With the mass production of many thousands of bottles for the perfume industry ensuring commercial success for his factory, Lalique was able to further his artistic ambitions in producing other decorative items for use as dressing table accessories. Distinctive bottles were on sale in his Paris shop for use as reusable containers: they were sold empty, to be filled with perfume from smaller, plain, disposable containers. Some of these bottles, particularly the larger ones, had stoppers which were designed for use as droppers. Other unique containers of this period were bowls for face powder. Many were decorated with distinctive open-headed maroon anemones which combine typical art nouveau and art deco decorative features. Most of these dressing table accessories are marked with an engraved or moulded Lalique signature.

As the Great War drew to a close, fashion design underwent a transformation, the art nouveau style beginning to be ousted by the new designs of art

deco. With the arrival of the twenties, women had much more of a voice in the fashion styles created for them. Perfume became an essential accessory on the dressing tables of most middle-class women of elegance. As art deco became the new vogue, Lalique demonstrated the full measure of his versatility, his designs taking on more rectangular shapes. He continued to be recognized as the leading designer of perfume bottles, his products and designs sought after by most of the leading perfumers in France. In fact the perfume bottles which became such an important part of the Lalique factory turnover are still being made to this day.

In 1924, for example, the House of Worth commissioned Lalique to create a special perfume bottle for their new fragrance 'Dans la Nuit'. Lalique designed a spherical bottle moulded with a star decoration in plain or frosted blue glass. The name of the perfume was moulded on the disc-shaped stopper. Such was the success of this perfume that Lalique was commissioned to design other Worth perfume bottles. In order to reduce costs, these were constructed in a simpler form than those of other perfumers, and were manufactured by Lalique in their thousands. Interestingly, in 1933 Worth manufactured a unique blue perfume, called 'Je

Above: 'Sirenes' perfume bottle. The mermaid was one of Lalique's favourite motifs and appears on bowls, hanging lights and many small items

Reviens'. This was presented in a tall, fluted blue bottle with a tiered neck and a round turquoise stopper, a classical art deco design. Another Worth perfume, 'Sans Adieu', was sold in a rectangular green bottle with a spiral 'worm-head' stopper. 'Impudence' featured yet another art deco design of clear circular glass in a spiral shape with a rounded stopper. Other delightful names for these perfumes included 'Mystère', 'Coeur de Joie', 'Pavots d'Argent', 'La Belle Saison' and 'Canarina'.

Many glass collectors spend a lifetime in the pursuit of these fine Lalique perfume bottles. An elegant, slim bottle in a frosted amber colour on which are sculpted several sleekly robed maidens was designed for a perfume with the attractive name of 'L'Ambre Antique', and is now a particularly collectable item. Many bottles bore a serial number which corresponded with the number of the stopper, enabling today's collectors to ascertain easily whether a bottle still has its original stopper. It was not long, however, before stoppers were replaced by atomizers and squeeze bulbs.

During the mid-1920s there was a brief resurgence of interest in articles decorated in the oriental style and Lalique was not slow to produce some bottles sculpted in a dull green glass which emulated Chinese snuff bottles of green jade, with carving which is uncannily similar to early Ming designs of intertwining tendrils and lotus flowers.

Imitating Lalique

Many of the more unusual of Lalique's scent bottles were exhibited at the Paris Exposition des Arts Décoratifs et Industriels in 1925. This exhibition demonstrated to the world the supremacy of French design and gave rise to the term 'art deco'. By now demand for Lalique's glassware was so great that other glassmakers soon began to copy and forge his works, and these imitations flooded the stores and boutiques of France. Lalique's fame and popularity was recognized not only by French glass-makers such as Sabino, and Genet et Michon who sometimes simply stamped their copies of Lalique 'Made in France', but also by manufacturers abroad who similarly attempted to imitate his wares. Factories in Czechoslovakia produced many bowls and vases in direct competition with Lalique's frosted glassware, though many of these were moulded in a heavy chunky style and in no way came near the artistry of Lalique's glass.

Factories in England were not slow to attempt to emulate Lalique's success either. The firm of Jobling introduced a range called 'Opalique' which even played on the Lalique name, a significant back-handed compliment. Davidson's made a range termed 'cloud glass' which was obviously inspired by the marbled effects of Lalique's *pâte de verre* work. Although these imitations infuriated Lalique, he met the challenge head on by making his products ever more difficult to copy: his glassware designs of the later 1920s became still more detailed in their sculpted techniques, forcing imitators to work doubly hard and setting them a virtually impossible task.

As unusual object on sale in Lalique's Paris showrooms in the late 1920s was a perfume burner. This comprised a frosted glass dome upon a heavy glass base which had a sculpted floral decoration, with the centres of the flowers cut out to allow the burning perfume to escape. Its shape is typically art deco, yet at the same time it displays a classical simplicity. Other perfume burners of opalescent glass were carved with animals, insects and flowers. A favourite one, called 'Papillons', had carved butterflies under a removable dome-shaped cover.

From the beginnings of his venture into glass-making and from the time of his opening of the glassworks at Combs La Ville, Lalique had always geared his glass manufacturing towards mass production, realizing that producing isolated masterpieces was not commercially viable. His products were pressed, blown and cast on a very large scale. Although he did not entirely abandon his *cire perdue* methods in the making of glass, these were relegated to the background. His aim was to make articles for the home that were both functional and

Below: *A round powder box and cover. The cover bears a fish design, another of Lalique's favourite motifs. 8 cm 3$\frac{1}{4}$ in in diameter*

Above: Two glass pendants flank one of the commemorative medallions which Lalique made to mark an exhibition at his Place Vendôme showrooms in 1912

aesthetically pleasing, and within the price range of the middle and lower middle class. Lalique realized only too well that production costs and wastage during experimentation were far too high. Thus while he recognized the artistic abilities of the *maître verrier*, Emile Gallé, who had been France's leading glass-maker until his death in 1904, at the same time that Lalique was acclaimed as the country's leading jeweller, he did not waste much time in attempting to emulate Gallé's achievements.

In 1911 Lalique ceased making expensive individual jewellery items altogether. In 1912, three years after opening his factory at Combs La Ville, he held an exhibition of his new art forms in glass at his showrooms on the Place Vendôme. He made commemorative invitations in the form of circular glass medallions with moulded lettering to commemorate the event. These measured about 7 cm ($2\frac{3}{4}$ in) in diameter and were green in colour. On their reverse was a design of sprigs of mistletoe with berries carved in relief. These were direct descendants of Lalique's small bronze plaques and medallions made to commemorate his jewellery exhibitions in the late 1890s and early 1900s. They represent some of the most collectable pieces by Lalique and fetch extremely high prices in the leading international salerooms.

Dressing table accessories

As well as exhibiting some specially designed perfume bottles at this private exhibition in 1912, Lalique included many other articles of glassware, including dressing-table *garnitures*; these elegant small glass boxes in various colours, made to contain not only powder, but small pins and pieces of jewellery and other articles necessary for a lady's toilette, were extremely popular and an essential adornment of a lady's boudoir at that time. Many *garnitures* were elegantly marketed in satin- and silk-lined boxes which gave them an extra distinctive quality.

Black was a popular colour for glass on a lady's dressing table and many small pomade holders with etched decoration on their lids were moulded in black glass. Sometimes the bases of the powder boxes were made of metal and occasionally Lalique designed the base of cardboard, a clear indication that the item was intended to be disposable and replaced when empty. Other exhibits included small glass articles for use as desk and writing accessories such as paperweights, seals, inkwells and blotters. Glass seals measuring between 9–10 cm ($3\frac{1}{2}$–4 inches) high, proved popular with his customers. Many were of frosted glass with the name 'Lalique' etched in Roman letters on to the side of the base. Sometimes Lalique sculpted

Below: *Lalique made a wide range of boxes. This one is in black glass and silvered bronze. The hinges and clasp are in the form of a scarab*

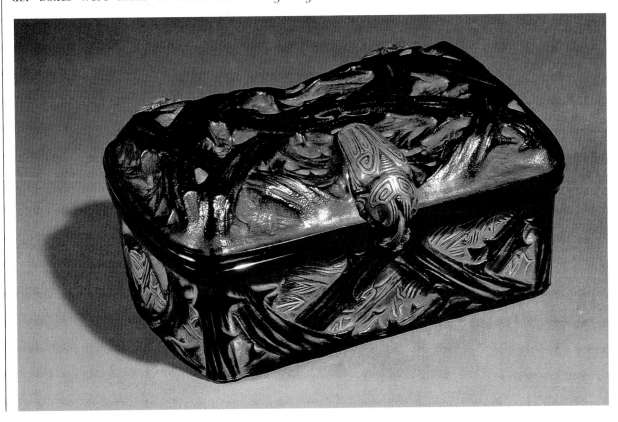

63

Above: *'Tête d'aigle' (Eagle's head) seal in black glass. 7.8 cm 3 in. Most of Lalique's seals have animals or birds as their subjects*

tiny animals on top and these bear an uncanny resemblance to some of his carved jewellery creations, and to many of the Japanese *netsuke* ivory carvings. One paperweight which illustrates yet again the influence of oriental craftsmanship on Lalique consists of a plain rectangular piece of glass with incised corners and two lizards, side by side and

head to tail, sculpted in high relief. This example of carving is much evidenced in Japanese shakudo work on *tsuba*.

Lalique made a few black glass boxes which measured some 19 × 10 cm ($7\frac{1}{2}$ × 4 inches). These were decorated with a symmetrical wheel-cut pattern of a sharp-thorned briar branch. They had hinged lids held in place by a silver-plated brass clasp carved in the shape of a scarab beetle with incised folded wing decoration. These *objets de vertu* are artistically quite outstanding. Their design is simple and yet they exhibit typical Japanese characteristics. The use of black gives the object a striking, even grotesque, appearance, reminiscent in many ways of Lalique's jewellery of the 1890s.

Other requisites of a lady's dressing table were hand mirrors, and Lalique designed these with bronze or silver frames carved with animal and plant forms. He also made a large selection of decanters, carafes, jugs and drinking glasses, relatively simple in design with little ornamentation, and inexpensive enough to be aimed at a mass market. Even at this early date he had the business acumen to keep his prices for functional objects highly competitive.

It was at the 1912 exhibition that Lalique also first demonstrated his consummate skill in turning a functional vase into an article of such outstanding beauty that, even today, almost every collector associates the name of Lalique with vases in particular. The excellence of his design and manufacture of vases in terms of their shape, colour and decorative qualities was quite outstanding.

The vases exhibited in 1912 were only a small representational example of what Lalique was to produce in later years. Most of these early exhibits were mould-blown, a technique which involved blowing the glass by means of the mouth or a pair of bellows into a hinged double mould. Sometimes they were made in sections and could therefore be reproduced fairly easily, although it is evident that some of the relief carving was hand-applied.

A few of these early vases displayed characteristics which Lalique employed in his jewellery pieces. The decoration encompassed the use of unusual and startling motifs which were somehow given even greater emphasis when modelled upon a glass base. These were made using the *cire perdue* method, by which, as we have seen, a solid model was carved in wax and encased in a refractory clay which was allowed to harden. The whole model was heated gently, which allowed the wax to melt away through a prepared aperture. Because the finished product was to be a hollow container, the molten glass was carefully blown into the mould and after cooling and annealing, the master mould was destroyed and the finished product removed. The manufacture of these vessels required a high degree

Below: *A black glass powder box. Height 8.5 cm 3½ in. Black was popular for dressing table accessories before 1914*

Above: *A cire perdue glass vase with a design of grotesque bullheaded fish around the base. 19.5 cm 7¾ in. This vase was made in 1923*

of skill, and some were modelled by Lalique himself. Because they were not made in large numbers, but only for exhibition purposes or as special commissions for wealthy clients, they are extremely valuable and fetch enormous sums on their rare appearances in the world's leading auction houses.

After the Great War

As a result of the fall in the production of glass during the Great War the glassworks at Combs La Ville was closed in 1915 and reopened in 1919 when demand for luxury articles in Western Europe and the United States increased dramatically. Lalique was not slow in meeting this demand with his innovatory designs. He soon realized that he needed a larger, more modern factory and in 1919, with the aid of a government grant, he purchased a site at Wingen sur Moder in the region of

Bas Rhin in Alsace, near the German border. Alsace was a former German province which had become French upon the cessation of hostilities in 1918. The factory was completed in 1921 and Lalique, now sixty years of age, with a reputation which was now established and recognized worldwide, entered upon a further stage of his distinguished career.

From the very beginning, output at the Wingen sur Moder factory was geared almost exclusively to mass production. Lalique was determined that his glass products should reach the widest market possible. He began to achieve his aim by extending his marketing activities, appointing agents and supplying high-class retail establishments in North America and in some of the capital cities of South America as well as throughout Western Europe. His range was vast, including almost every conceivable type of glass object. He lost no opportunity to display his factory products at international exhibitions. Museums and galleries were encouraged to have special showings of Lalique artefacts.

In order to understand fully the tremendous changes in fashion and style which took place in Europe after the Great War, it is important to realize that the war provided a new independence for women who had at last succeeded in achieving complete emancipation. While their men were away fighting, women had been working in jobs that had previously been an exclusively male domain. Now women began to dominate the dictates of fash-

Above: 'Deux chèvres' (Two goats), a circular mirror in frosted, clear and blue stained glass. 16 cm $6\frac{1}{4}$ in. The central handle is moulded with fruiting vines

ion, interior design and all aspects of decorative art. A mood of flamboyance hit America and Europe, the redistribution of wealth created a large clientele with money to spend and exotic tastes not only in couture, perfumery and jewellery, but also in a new type of home and its furnishings.

'Victoire', one of Lalique's most sought after car mascots

Chapter Three

THE ART DECO YEARS

The Great War transformed the fabric of European society from top to bottom. With his customary ability, René Lalique anticipated the changes that this would mean and, opening a second glass factory in 1921, was ready to cater for the demands of the machine age. Using industrial methods, but without any loss of quality, he produced relatively inexpensive pieces of glass jewellery, a host of modestly priced functional items, including plates and bowls, jugs, decanters and drinking glasses, inkwells and ash trays, vases and light fittings in the new art deco style, a series of stunning car mascots – symbols of the age of speed – and many more supremely crafted examples of the glass-maker's art.

While the movements which created the art nouveau school had emphasized the individuality of artists and deplored the use of the machine, art deco actively encouraged the use of new technology to meet insatiable public demand. Artefacts of good quality and good craftsmanship were needed to satisfy as many people as possible. Art deco *was* the age of the machine. It encompassed almost every facet of living, and all items in the areas of furniture, fashion, architecture, advertising, printing, interior design, pottery, porcelain and glass underwent a total transformation in terms of shape and decoration.

Lalique understood the change of mood and planned his productions accordingly. He foresaw the period of frivolity which was coming – the Roaring Twenties, with the Flapper and La Garçonne, both of whom had a totally new set of requirements. Bright colours were 'in'. Electric zigzag and sunburst patterns with geometric friezes predominated in many designs.

Lalique's mass-produced range in the relatively inexpensive material of glass included brooches, bracelets, pendants, necklaces, pins, buckles, rings, cufflinks and buttons. A great deal of his jewellery was made of press-moulded clear glass and set on a metal mount covered

Above: *Glass brooches with gilt-metal mounts, circa 1920. Clockwise from top left, the subjects are moths, frogs, a coiled serpent, a grotesque mask and three monkfish*

70

in thin, coloured metal foil which reflected an iridescent light. Sometimes the resulting effect is similar to the *plique à jour* enamelling technique Lalique employed earlier in his career. The iridescent sheen on some of the brooches recalls the changing colours of the wings of the butterflies and dragonflies that he created during his art nouveau period, and the simple device of employing a metal foil to produce the effect was relatively inexpensive. Many of these metal mounts have a Lalique mark on their reverse.

Lalique's shapes reflected the craze for geometric patterns, and his jewellery was often square-cut. His rings often had a bombé shape in the art deco style. Some of the pendants and necklaces consisted of press-moulded coloured and opalescent glass shapes strung on knotted cords with silk tassels. Occasionally Lalique also made necklaces of a more exclusive nature for sale in his Place Vendôme showrooms to his more discerning and wealthy clients. Some of these more sophisticated designs emulated rock crystal and were quite expensive.

Glass made to represent coloured pebbles and mounted on gilt metal as a brooch was particularly attractive and popular. Sometimes a pendant would feature a large piece of moulded and coloured glass in the shape of a thick 'T', or a shield or cross bearing sculpted decoration in the art nouveau manner; a curious mixture of the art nouveau and art deco styles. Lalique made bracelets of different coloured beads strung together on elastic bands; these were

Above: *Glass brooches with gilt-metal mounts, made circa 1920. From the top the subjects are a stylised rose briar, cicadas, thistles and birds of prey*

aimed at the lower end of the market. Necklaces were sometimes made in extraordinary lengths which could wind around a lady's neck four or five times. Occasionally sets of six or eight buttons were specially made in coloured glass, each bearing an impressed Lalique mark.

Once again Lalique derived inspiration from Japanese craftsmen, as he had around the turn of the century, for many of his glass pendants are obviously direct copies of *tsuba*, even to the extent of including the *kozuda* and *kogai* holes of the sword guards and utilizing them as accessories for threading through a hanging cord, sometimes with a silken tassel adornment. These pendants were made in many colours and some are moulded in varying shades of brown, again emulating Japanese craftsmanship. The sculpted glass decoration skilfully imitates the art of metal carving.

All these items of jewellery were produced in large quantities throughout the 1920s at Lalique's new factory at Wingen sur Moder in what is now the département of Bas-Rhin, near the border with Germany, as were many thousands of other glass artefacts.

***Below left:** A frosted glass and enamel pendant with a design of gleaming fish on a subtly coloured background. It was made in about 1925. 5 cm 2 in*

***Below right:** An electric blue glass pendant of rounded triangular form, moulded with two trailing lily blooms, on a blue silk cord. 5.3 cm 2$\frac{1}{8}$ in*

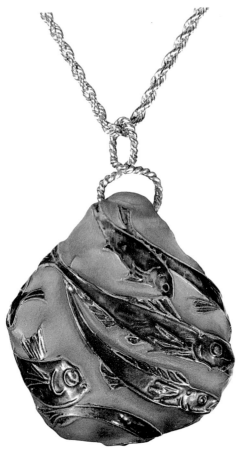

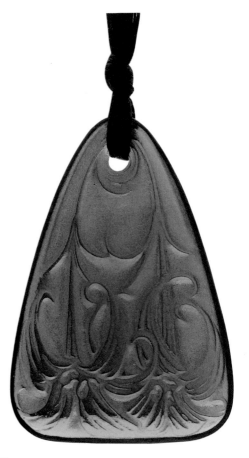

Car mascots

This was the decade of speed, epitomized by the rapid expansion of the motor car and aeroplane industries. Speed became almost a drug; anyone who was anybody owned a motorcar and it was natural that owners should want to personalize their prize possession, to distinguish it in some marked way and make it uniquely their own. What better status symbol than a car mascot?

Lalique was not in fact the inventor of the car mascot. The earliest example is claimed to be English in origin and to date back to the later years of the 19th century. It was, however, in America that the idea first caught on before being copied by French and English mascot-makers. The early mascots were sculpted in bronze, chromium plate and base metals. Their popularity was such that it was not long before Lalique created the first of his car mascots in glass. These are highly prized collector's items today.

The majority of motor cars in the 1920s and 1930s had a radiator cap with a screw-fitting metal attachment which was ideally suited as a mount for a car mascot. Sometimes the mascot was mounted further back over the engine casings and bolted into place.

One of Lalique's earliest mascots featured a dragonfly and was called 'Libellule'. It was made of frosted glass with veined wings pointing skywards. Under the bronze base a multi-coloured lighted disc was attached to the car dynamo. The disc revolved when the car was moving at speed, giving differ-

Above: 'Grande Libellule', a frosted and polished car mascot modelled as a dragonfly with its wings vertically extended. Height 20.5 cm 8 in

ent intensities of light which cast rainbow shades through the body of the insect. As the speed of the car increased, so the colours changed, creating a magical firefly effect of multi-coloured splendour.

In all Lalique made over twenty-five different car mascots, many serving a dual purpose as a paperweight. There were several different grasshopper designs, the proud head of a peacock, a cockerel, an eagle, a falcon, a pair of horses, a frog, a mermaid and a ram's head, all exquisitely designed and each a unique work of art. Some mascots were manufactured in the shape of circular

Above: 'Saint-Christophe', a car mascot in clear glass with a satin finished intaglio design of St Christopher, the patron saint of travellers. Height 13.0 cm 5⅛ in

medallions with a St Christopher or an archer in intaglio form. Many of the mascots were designed to express the notion of speed. One particularly beautiful one, called 'Vitesse', featured a nude figure of a nymph leaning backwards as though pushed by the wind. Another design, the 'Comète', was distinctly art deco in shape, consisting of a star with geometrically fan-shaped lines spreading from the base to form a tail that simulated speed. The most popular of Lalique's car mascots was a model called 'Victoire'. This represented a woman's head, chin straining forward and mouth open, the hair streaming backwards and slightly upwards in straight geometric lines as though held by the wind. This was one of Lalique's finest designs epitomizing the age of speed, and succeeded more than any other of his creations in capturing the 1920s notion of using the female form as a design element in the art deco manner. It symbolized the jazz age and was a fitting figurehead to project the image of emancipated womanhood. 'Victoire' was used on the most expensive cars and given the fitting name of 'Spirit of the Wind' by many English customers.

Lalique was specially commissioned to design some car mascots for the French Citroën Automobile Company including 'Cinq Chevaux', which featured five prancing horses in clear glass, carved closely, one upon the other, and it was not long before other glass and crystal makers in the United States as well as Europe began to copy his designs. These imitations did not match the artistry of Lalique's products, however, being more heavily moulded and lacking his crispness of detail in the carving. All these mascots were designed to have a fitted light bulb in the base if the customer required, and were advertised in many leading motor magazines. Car mascots were regularly advertised in the catalogues of Lalique's London agents, the Breves Galleries, priced from three to seven guineas plus an extra guinea if fitted with a light bulb. Today they sometimes feature in special sales of Lalique glass and often reach four figure sums, a fitting tribute to Lalique's artistic ability.

All these car mascots bore the signature 'R. Lalique', engraved on the base or moulded upon the side of the model. They continued to be made well into the 1930s. The *Studio* magazine for February 1931 included a feature on Lalique's car mascots and stated that 'a car figure head is essentially an item of decor as much so as a glittering ornament in a lady's hat'. Most of them are made in clear glass, sometimes highlighted with black staining in the crevices of the mould. Coloured models are rare: an unusual one is of a perch in orange-yellow opalescent glass.

As motor car manufacturers began to develop their own particular car logo as mascots, so Lalique simply changed the function of his mascots, making them into paperweights and bookends, and many continued to be manufactured and sold as desk accessories and ornaments.

Right: *'Vitesse', a car mascot in frosted glass of a naked female figure, personifying speed. Height 18.8 cm 7½ in*

Overleaf (left): *'Tête de Coq', a car mascot in clear amethyst glass. 18 cm 7¼ in*

Overleaf (right); *'Cinq Chevaux'. One of Lalique's first car mascots, this design was commissioned by Citroën for their 5CV model in 1925. 11 cm 4⅜ in.*

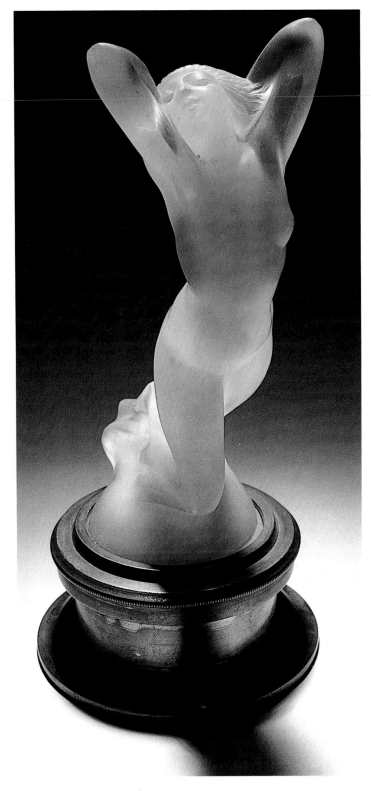

Marc Lalique

From the time of the opening of his glassworks at Wingen sur Moder, Lalique's output increased enormously. The factory was equipped with the very latest machinery, which included the use of steel moulds. Much of the credit for the success of this increased production must go to Lalique's son Marc, who joined the company shortly after the opening of the works at Wingen. Whereas René was the inspiration and creative genius behind all the factory production, Marc contributed a high degree of technical skill to the engineering problems of mass-producing glass artefacts. He was particularly interested in the processes of cooling and annealing, when a glass object is most vulnerable to losing its shape and crack-ing. He experimented widely and successfully invented several new methods of glass moulding and blowing. Many of his ideas were patented, and although the creative genius of his father was never undermined, Marc played an important part on the manufacturing side in bringing his father's works to the attention of an international public.

Below left: 'Senlis', this clear grey glass vase in the 'Sophora' shape with bronze handles in the form of stylised leaves, is very scarce. 26 cm 10¼ in

Below right: 'Moissac', this vase with a design of leaves in an unusual gun-metal colour and satin finish, has a silver band around the rim. Approx. 20 cm 8 in

Vases

Some of René Lalique's earlier vase creations were identical in shape and made by the mould-blown process, acquiring individuality only from the carved and moulded decoration which was later grafted on to the blank body of the vase. The cost of producing the blank bodies in large numbers was not high, but Lalique found that the processes of adding moulded decoration involved more and more costly production work, which was why he did not pursue this method of manufacture.

Among examples of the blank vases produced was one called 'Sophora'. It was a narrow-necked vase with a bulbous body of frosted grey patinated glass decorated with a highly polished raised leaf decoration. The overall effect is very similar to Chinese lacquer decoration which is sometimes deeply carved, revealing different coloured

Above: 'Languedoc', a vase with a frosted finish, moulded in high relief with overlapping leaves. 22.5 cm 9 in

layers. The 'Sophora' shape was also used in one of Lalique's most original moulded blank vase creations which he called 'Senlis', see illustration opposite. The body of the vase was retained in its blank state with no embellishment or decoration added apart from two thick handles sculpted from bronze in the Greek amphora style. These handles were cast in the factory foundry, then placed upon the shoulders and body of the vase. Glass vases with bronze handles are very rare.

Among the vases produced in the first year of the Wingen factory are some of the largest that Lalique ever made, measuring as high as 43 cm (17 inches). They proved particularly

popular with the interior designers of the day, being impressive enough to reflect the richness and elegance of the new art deco furnishings which wealthy people were demanding.

Most of Lalique's vases were given attractive names which, like his perfume bottle labels, proved to have distinct marketing advantages. A typical example of the larger pieces of work was called 'Palestre'. This vase featured a wheel-cut decoration of nude male figures sculpted in the style of Greek gods or athletes in pale lavender frosted glass. Another very popular vase, made in many sizes and many colours, was called 'Sauterelles' (grasshoppers): it had a bulbous shape with embossed trailing intertwining branches support-

Above: The unusual 'Nanking' vase, height 33.7 cm 13¼ in, and an 'Oranges' vase in enamelled glass, height 29 cm 11½ in

ing numerous grasshoppers. Sometimes this vase was moulded and produced in a single colour, while in some models the green patination of the grasshopper contrasts with a different coloured background.

Press-moulding

One of the most important engineering innovations to take place at the Wingen sur Moder works in its early days, concerned the development of the technique of press-moulding. This revolutionary concept of moulding glass became a standard method of production in the Lalique factory and has been continued until the present day. The process was economical and far less complicated than blow-moulding, resulting in a smaller number of 'wasters', and was therefore an important contributory factor in keeping Lalique's products very competitively priced. Press-moulding involved introducing the molten glass directly into the metal moulds where it was forced into the required shape by means of a vertical plunger, usually operated manually on a lever system. In order to allow the easy entry and withdrawal of the metal plunger from the mould, the mouth of the hollow vessel had of necessity to be the widest part. Thus press-moulded vases are characterized by a downward tapering shape which is in marked contrast with the bulbous, narrow-necked, blow-moulded products. Also, because of the extreme pressure of the plunger, the glass had a crispness of sculpted relief which was not easily achieved by means of the blown method of manufacture. The *Studio* of August 1924 stated that 'Lalique is raising moulded glass to a level which it has never before attained. By employing his moulds after the same fashion as a modeller in bronze employs those of a piece of sculpture, Lalique secures effects similarly sculpturesque and opens up possibilities hitherto unexplored in this connection.' The new method of press-moulding played a considerable part, too, in Lalique's development of architectural glass panel production.

Above: 'Sauterelles' (Grasshoppers). This vase, which dates from the 1920s, was made in a variety of colours and in both clear and frosted glass. Height 25.5 cm 10 in

Overleaf left: 'Martin Pecheurs' (Kingfishers), a black ovoid vase with kingfishers perched on flowering branches. Height 23.5 cm $9\frac{1}{4}$ in

Overleaf right: 'Bacchantes'. This magnificent vase with its frieze of naked maidens in high relief was still in production in the 1970s. Height 25 cm 10 in

Above: 'Bresse'. A glass vase of bulbous shape with a wide lip. The body bears a stylized design in amber and grey. Height 10 cm 4 in

The diversity of shapes, colours, sizes and decorative designs of Lalique's vases was truly vast, and each had distinctive features and style that were instantly recognized as bearing the hallmark of a master. Although almost all Lalique's glass was clearly marked with his name in moulded relief or etched upon the body or base, this was by now almost superfluous. Lalique's glasswork is so distinctive and so fine that it is usually instantly recognizable.

René Lalique was responsible for the design of over 200 vases during the 1920s and 1930s, all exhibiting individual characteristics and showing no evidence of any copying or adaptation of previous designs. Their quality remained consistent even though by now Lalique was beginning to suffer from the debilitating disease of arthritis in his hands. That the range of his articles in glass showed no signs of diminishing because of this condition can be seen as an amazing achievement when one considers that every item in the enormous output from the Lalique factory was originally designed and made by the master himself.

Light fittings

It was during the 1920s that Lalique first seriously applied his talent to the art of designing lighting fixtures, although in the magazine *L'Art Décoratif* in 1905 there was an illustration of a chandelier by him consisting of a bronze mount into which glass had been blown to form a shade, with lizards sculpted in high relief. Other illustrations of Lalique's work in this medium were published in *Art et Décoration* in 1906, including two other unusual lighting fixtures. One, a lantern, had twelve bronze chameleons alternately facing head to tail, holding the lantern's glass panels. The animals had the grotesque, startling appearance of much of Lalique's art nouveau jewellery: their predatory eyes and spiked tails are poised as if ready to pounce on the unwary passer-by.

Another chandelier fixing was also fashioned in bronze, this time with a dragonfly decoration in enamelled crystal around the circular mounting. This was strikingly similar to Lalique's famous dragonfly corsage jewellery. He also made a circular hanging fixture

of clear glass showing eight flying insects' wings with heavily etched decoration to simulate the veins.

All these, however, were early isolated examples. They were meant to be more *objets de vertu* than functional. At this time Lalique was more involved with his jewellery and *objets de vertu* and no doubt he realized that many light fittings designed in the art nouveau style by such masters as Emile Gallé and August and Antonin Daum of the Nancy School were receiving international acclaim, with which he had no desire to compete commercially.

However, as the twentieth century progressed, lighting became increasingly important, and it was soon realized that glass, with its light-diffusing qualities, was the ideal medium to

Right: A chandelier in clear and frosted glass, moulded in high relief with a design of leaves and birds. 1920s. 37 cm 14½ in square, 94 cm 37 in overall height

Left: 'Aljer'. A rare, large chandelier with eight plaques of clear and frosted glass, moulded in intaglio with birds holding fruiting swags. Height 71 cm 28 in

provide artificial illumination. Art deco demanded that light should be achromatic and utilized to illuminate home interiors in a functional way. This was a complete reversal of the art nouveau emphasis on the lamps themselves as the focus of attraction. Gone now were the coloured, heavily overlaid lamps with shades of sculpted ornamental bronze-

work. Glass was now to be used to orchestrate light, and by the skilful use of enamelling and etching, varying shades of light could be achieved. Lalique realized that he could obtain such nuances with sculpted glass effects. The degree of light intensity need not be lost by the addition of a sculpted or etched decoration; indeed it could be improved by diffusion through such glass. He began to manufacture glass light fixtures on a commercial scale at the Wingen factory in the 1920s.

The fixtures included chandeliers, hanging lamps, wall brackets, table lamps and illuminated statuettes. Lalique even made illuminated glass tables as well as many objects for architectural use, including wall panels, friezes and

Above: *'Oiseau de feu' (Firebird) surtout of moulded clear and frosted glass, with a bronze illuminating stand carved with moths. Height 43 cm 17¼ in*

Opposite: *This table lamp with a horseshoe-shaped shade in cherry blossom design is reminiscent of the scent bottles with tiara stoppers (page 50). 41 cm 18 in*

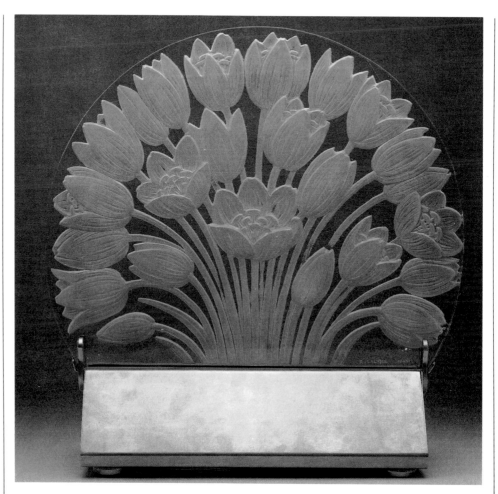

ceiling tiles. His night lights or *luminaires* incorporated features of both his perfume burners and his tiara-stoppered scent bottles. They consisted of a central dome-shaped cover, usually made of fluted frosted glass, which held the light bulb, with a decorative parabola in a tiara shape. These parabolas bore finely etched decorations of cherry blossom branches, putti amidst trailing flower decoration, a flight of swallows or sprays of roses. Particularly attractive were pairs of love-birds perched on flowering branches. These night lights gave little illumination and were prob-

Above: *'Tulipes'. A clear and frosted* luminaire *of demi-lune form, moulded with a fan-shaped bouquet of tulips. The metal base encloses the light fitting. 47 cm 18½ in*

ably intended as decorative accessories for use on the dressing table in a lady's bedroom.

As lamps became less decorative and more functional in their use, it soon became clear that the dazzling intensity of a naked light bulb was not necessarily the best way of utilizing this new form of illumination. Reflecting light from a

secondary source, such as a ceiling or wall, succeeded in softening its intensity. The change from direct to indirect lighting resulted in many more fittings designed to reflect light upwards or sideways.

Some of Lalique's early table lamps, although designed in the art deco shape, still displayed decorative features which incorporated the use of motifs not far removed from those of the art nouveau school. He sometimes employed the peacock design which he had favoured for many years. It was not long, however, before he developed the

Above: 'Coquilles'. Lalique used the clam shell motif on bowls, vases and other tableware, as well as for hanging light fittings

simplicity of line and sobriety of decoration which contemporary art deco designers were applying to all manner of functional items. Some had shades of an inverted bowl shape intended to provide indirect light by upward reflection, while many took on the favourite geometric shapes of the art deco period, with outlines of streamlined simplicity.

Lalique followed other light designers in his use of chromium-plated metal stands, and hollow metal tubes to contain and conceal the electric wires in his designs. His catalogue of this period displayed over twenty different table lamp patterns.

As the demand for purely functional lighting fixtures increased, Lalique made wall and ceiling lights shaped in the form of circular bowls for fitting directly on to a wall or hanging from a ceiling. He also designed quarter and semi-circular bowls called *appliques* to attach to the walls and corners of a room. He created many different designs moulded in varying thicknesses, producing tonal gradations of light intensity. Most of these *appliques* were made in clear or opalescent glass, some with patina highlights. They all bore a simple engraved decoration in art deco geometric style. A favourite motif was a series of carved scallop shells emanating into a fan shape from the centre of the light fitting or dish.

Lalique's chandeliers differed from other suspended light fittings in one major respect: they did not have facet-cut glass which projected a maximum amount of light by its reflective qualities. All Lalique's chandeliers utilized the properties of translucency created within the glass itself. Most of his chandeliers were made of frosted glass, an ideal medium for transmitting warmth and radiance. An interesting feature of Lalique's chandeliers was the use of a glass sleeve or tube decorated with grooved patterns to conceal the electric wiring and hanging chains. Sometimes the chandeliers were branched and Lalique fashioned shades in the shape of flower heads, which were also designed to conceal where the chandelier was fitted to the ceiling.

Below: *A pair of opalescent hemispherical wall lights, moulded with stylised sunbursts with centres in high relief. Circa 1930. Width 30.5 cm 12 in*

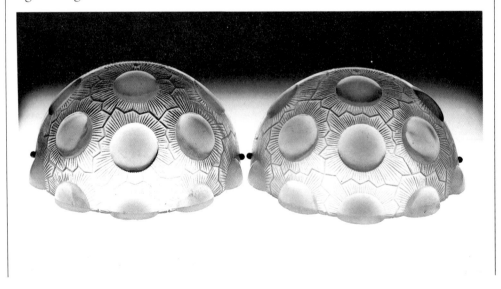

These chandeliers were rarely sold to private customers but were more often purchased for use in hotels and shops.

Sculpted glass

The facilities of the factory at Wingen allowed Lalique to develop fully his technique of casting glass in sculptural form. Shortly after the opening at Wingen he produced a pair of statuettes which were outstanding examples of his carving ability. These models, each 23 cm (9 inches) high, representing female nudes, called 'Suzanne' and 'Thaïs', were ideal for use as ornamental lighting objects because of their frosted opalescent translucency. Each sculpted figure stood with one foot bent slightly backwards, arms outstretched to hold a diaphanous gown with softly sculpted folds falling around a rectangular base. They were sold with illuminating stands of decorated bronze or plain metal which permitted the transmission of light from underneath and behind the statuette, creating a graceful and sensual effect and projecting an image of limpidity and richness.

Illuminated vases and plaques

Lalique sometimes used vases for the purpose of illumination, as well as a series of plaques made of fairly thick brightly polished clear glass in a fan shape and decorated with frosted glass figures. They were sold in conjunction with a metal or bronze base to contain the lighting fixture. These illuminated plaques, known as *surtouts*, were not, however, ideal for the transmission of light. They were intended more as

Above: 'Suzanne'. *This statuette was made for at least 10 years from 1922. It came in frosted, opalescent and coloured glass versions. Height 23 cm 9 in*

ornamental objects and were quite expensive. One of the largest and rarest of them, now worth a great deal of money, features a shallow fan shape over 90 cm (3 feet) wide. Standing on an illuminating base of sculpted bronze, the glass is decorated with three strutting peacocks, their tail feathers spreading in majestic folds to encompass the full width of the glass fan.

The 1925 Exposition

Lalique regularly showed glass made for lighting purposes at the annual Paris Salon Exhibitions. Examples of other Lalique lighting masterpieces were on display at the Exposition des Arts Décoratifs et Industriels in Paris in 1925. This international exhibition encompassed all the decorative arts and acted as a showcase for France's leading role in this field. It was at this exhibition that Lalique reached the pinnacle of his success. One of the most outstanding exhibits designed and made by him was staggering in its size and majesty. This was an enormous fountain over 15 metres (50 feet) high, designed as a centrepiece. It consisted of 17 tiers of frosted glass panels, each tier made of octagonal sections supported by 8 statuettes. The statuettes, which were called 'Sources de la Fontaine' came in 13 different versions of varying size. The basic model, which was moulded in frosted glass, portrayed a slim, maiden-like figure wearing a headdress whose folds fall over her shoulders to her feet in a beaded glass decoration. In her hands, emerging from the folds of her gown, she holds a fish. The statuette has qualities reminiscent of the Egyptian influence which was in evidence in Western Europe at that time, yet it also has madonna-like qualities.

Lalique was also commissioned to design the interiors for some of the pavilions at the exhibition. In fact almost every exhibitor showed something made by him, whether it was part

Above: *'Trois paons' (Three peacocks). This elaborate glass* surtout, *which has a bronze illuminating stand, was made in the late 1920s. Length 91.5 cm 36 in*

Opposite: *Two versions of the 'Source de la Fontaine' statuettes which Lalique made for the 1925 Paris Exposition. Height approx. 65.5 cm 26 in*

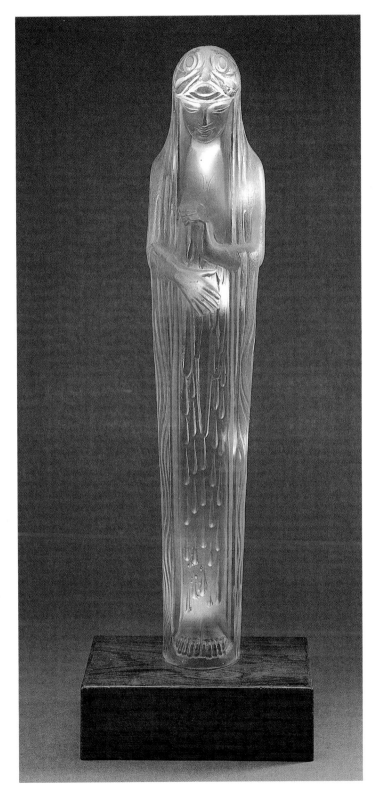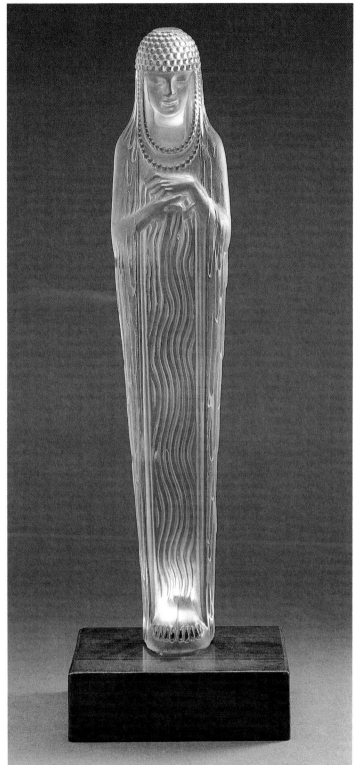

Above: *The fountain which Lalique designed for the Exposition des Art Decoratifs et Industriels in 1925. It was over 15 m 50 ft in height*

of the stand structure, for use as a container or just for decoration. Roger et Gallet used Lalique's talents to design the complete stand for their perfumes, including not only the perfume containers but also the showcase and the furniture. Other scent manufacturers also featured Lalique perfume bottles. Sèvres, the famous porcelain company, commissioned Lalique to design a complete dining room for them, with an illuminated ceiling made from frosted glass. This proved highly successful and was widely acclaimed.

Lalique's talent in the design of light fittings was fully utilized throughout the showrooms and setting of the exhibition. Large frosted glass panels stood either side of the entrance doors and his big illuminated vases featured prominently as decorative items throughout the pavilions and stands of the numerous exhibitors. Lalique himself had a small showroom at the exhibition, where he exhibited his commercial glass. His tablewares and vases were universally acclaimed and it was at this exhibition that he introduced a vase called 'Tourbillons' (Whirlwinds), measuring 20 cm (8 inches) in height and decorated with a deeply cut swirling motif reminiscent of a whirlwind. It was made in various colours including amber and the very popular electric blue. The vase was also available in clear glass, sometimes highlighted with black enamelling. Being mass-produced, it was available at a competitive price, although when examples appears nowadays in the salerooms they change hand for four figure sums.

Another vase shown at the exhibition was called the 'Serpent'. It was moulded in the shape of a coiled snake with sharply moulded scales and a widely flared mouth showing exposed fangs poised ready to strike. This vase, made in frosted glass, was available in various muted colour shades.

Lalique's small showroom at the exhibition, which he used to introduce many other new designs of functional items made in glass, was of stark design, with entrance doors made from over 2000 pieces of glass. The interior housed collections of his *cire perdue* glass in showcases which surrounded a magnificent vase which stood over 2 metres (6 feet) high in the middle of the showroom. It was constructed of moulded glass with designs of prancing horses and acanthus leaves in frosted panels.

Among the many *cire perdue* vases on show were some plain ovoid pieces with sculpted fish amidst waves, intricately cut away around the base. The modelling and carving again suggest a strong Japanese influence, reminiscent of the treatment of waves in the woodblock prints of Hiroshige and Hokusai.

Above: *'Serpent'. An amber glass vase of startlingly original design. Lalique also used the serpent motif in his art nouveau jewellery. Height 25 cm 9$\frac{7}{8}$ in*

Below: *'Tourbillons' (Whirlwinds). This dramatic, deeply moulded vase, which was made in clear and coloured glass, is highly sought after today. Height 20.5 cm 8 in*

After this exhibition, Lalique's reputation as a *maître verrier* as well as a *maître bijoutier* was established worldwide. This astonishing achievement of being acclaimed as a master in two very different media has never been equalled, let alone surpassed.

Functional objects

It must not be thought that all Lalique productions were expensive. The factories at Combs la Ville and Wingen sur Moder continued to mass-produce articles for a worldwide market. Many ordinary everyday functional items were in production during the 1920s and 1930s. These included ashtrays, bookends, inkwells, candlesticks, bonnières, menu-holders, place card-holders, condiment sets, pepper mills, knife rests, jardinières, shallow dishes, plates, bowls and mirrors.

Some of Lalique's toilet mirrors fashioned in clear glass are foil-backed. They have either square or circular frames, ornately decorated in frosted glass with sculpted floral or geometric patterns. They are very feminine in character and are among the most attractive useful items Lalique designed

Below: Lalique's 1932 catalogue listed 14 inkwells in a variety of shapes and sizes. This one, 'Trois Sirènes' (Three water sprites), measures 24 cm 9½ in in diameter

for use on a lady's dressing table.

As it became increasingly acceptable for women to smoke, Lalique extended his range of ashtrays for middle-class homes. They were mainly rectangular or circular, occasionally moulded with a leaf design or geometrically patterned relief. Some were of plain coloured glass with the figure of a small animal such as a dog or mouse, or a bird, moulded to form a handle placed in the centre. One ashtray had a plaque with a mermaid carved in a swirling pattern, a typical blend of art nouveau-inspired sculpture on an art deco-shaped dish.

Above: 'Deux Colombes' (Two doves). An opalescent clock, the circular glass face surmounted by two doves perched on a flowering prunus. Height 22.3 cm 8¾ in

Left: 'Le Jour et la Nuit' (Day and night). This clock, the most expensive Lalique made, came in several colours. Height 37.5 cm 14½ in

Some of Lalique's pieces were multi-purpose and were attached to different bases for varying functions, such as a bookend or paperweight. A peacock head was used for no fewer than four different items. An unusual group of objects consisted of about twenty different types of clock case. They were made in varying sizes for use on mantelpieces, tables and desks. The clock mechanisms were specially imported from Switzerland and bore the trade marks 'ATO'. Most of the cases were made in clear or opalescent glass with birds or flowers in sculpted relief.

An enormous quantity of tableware for everyday use was manufactured at Wingen after the 1925 exhibition. These pieces proved extremely popular and their prices were highly competitive. Among some of the articles in demand by a Lalique-conscious public were lemonade and wine sets consisting of six glasses with a carafe or decanter. Many of these sets were manufactured in a clear, moulded, orange-coloured glass, sometimes with the addition of a circular glass tray. The tablewares were made of crystal and had minimal decoration, usually just a little moulded relief applied around the stem or base of the bowl of each glass. Other drinking glasses which were much in demand in the 1920s and 1930s were flared, fan-shaped cocktail glasses. These were made in large numbers. Lalique even made swizzle sticks in sets of a dozen for fashionable customers who frequented the cocktail bars of Europe's top hotels and restaurants.

Much of Lalique's glassware was also supplied to international steamship and

Below: 'Grande Cyprins' (Large carp). An amber glass box with the base made of silk lined card. Circa 1925. 26 cm 10 in in diameter

railway companies and it is interesting to observe in this context that many of his drinking glasses were low-set on a flared base, a design intended to give the vessel better balance, for use in a moving railway restaurant car or on board ship in rough weather. He was commissioned to supply decanters, carafes and flagons to the firm of Cusenier, one of the leading retailers in the wine and spirit trade. Like Coty, Cusenier recognized the marketing advantages of selling well-packaged products and commissioned many of the finest glass-makers to manufacture containers for his wines and spirits. Lalique's special carafes and flagons were marketed by Cusenier all over the world.

Above: *'Hespérides'. An amber glass lemonade set comprising a jug, tumblers and tray, with a design of serrated leaves. The jug is 22 cm 8¼ in high*

One of the most functional and ordinary of objects to which Lalique's mastery of design was applied, and which is most often seen in sale rooms today, is the humble plate or shallow dish. As the manufacturing cost of producing shallow dishes or plates by a single pressing was basically low, they were made in very large numbers. Yet, on a visit to a saleroom, with perhaps a couple of hundred lots of mixed porcelain, pottery and glass on display, a Lalique plate

will instantly attract the eye by its colour and design. Many of the largest and more decorative were intended as serving plates. The designs created by Lalique were usually moulded on the underside of the dish and nearly always followed a radiating pattern emanating from the centre, although some are asymmetrical. The placing of the moulding in muted colour shades on the reverse of the plate produced a subtle luminosity through the opalescent glass, particularly if it was backlit.

There was enormous variation in the styles of moulded decoration. Some featured the classic art deco female nude in the centre of the plate standing in a sensuous pose with arms outstretched, asymmetrical branches of blossom flowing around the body to resemble a lighted Catherine wheel.

Above: A detail from 'Trepied sirène', an opalescent dish with three conical feet, showing a water nymph, a motif Lalique was to use again and again

Left: 'Calypso', an opalescent dish, moulded beneath the rim with five water nymphs of stylised art deco form. 30 cm 12 in in diameter

There were water nymphs and mermaid forms, too. One dish has five naiads placed in sensual curvilinear positions around the centre, their tails trailing towards the outer rim of the plate, depicting whirling eddies of water. A blue patina on these figures further creates a sense of water.

Some dishes were decorated with simple geometric circles and dots,

effects with extraordinary colour variations.

Many of these plates have the mark of 'R. Lalique. France' stencilled or engraved in the centre. These marks are not always easy to see and the dish has sometimes to be held at certain angles to the light for easier reading.

Most of Lalique's plates and dishes are made of fairly thick glass and are quite heavy. Their most appealing quality and most striking feature, apart from their outstanding pattern designs, is certainly their cloudy, milky colours.

Furniture

Lalique's unique versatility knew no bounds. He began to extend his interests from jewellery and glass design into furniture. Some of the tables he designed were typical of the art deco period, with their classic sharp outlines. Most of these were breakfast or dining tables intended to seat just four people. Being constructed almost entirely of glass, they were particularly good examples of the skill of the glass-makers at the Wingen sur Moder factory. Lalique first ventured into making tables around 1924–5 when he was asked to supply glass furniture for some of the exhibitors at the 1925 Paris Exposition. Although they did not represent a large proportion of the factory's output, he continued to manufacture glass tables

Above: *A photograph taken circa 1921 showing 'Hirondelles', a small clock decorated with five swallows against a background of flowering branches*

starting as small as 5 mm ($\frac{1}{4}$ inch) and gradually increasing in size as they reach the edge of the dish. Other favourite motifs included a shoal of fish, all with their heads in an asymmetrical pattern facing the centre of the dish, their tails swirling away into the rim; or tiny dots in the middle of the dish creating an impression of bubbling water. This, too, was often made in pale blue opalescent glass.

Moulded wheat-ears were also strongly favoured by Lalique in many of his 1920s designs. Perhaps the outstanding example of Lalique's ability to attract attention is the plate known as the 'Peacock Dish'. This has a radiating pattern of peacock 'eyes' on the feathers extending from the centre in increasing sizes. If placed near a light, the moulded decoration produced amazing reflective

up until the outbreak of World War II. Many of them were specially commissioned and some were designed to be illuminated from within, with special wiring attachments incorporated in the table legs. The table top was usually made of a specially thick piece of circular or square opalescent glass, decorated with a geometrical pattern or a frosted design. The table legs or supports were often of solid, vertically fluted glass set upon a solid glass base, sometimes supported by a framework of chromium plated metal. Occasionally these bases were coloured, giving a starkly contrasting effect with the illuminated glass.

Glass panels, plainly moulded with little or no decoration, were also used as a feature in the base structure of Lalique's tables.

As the 1930s progressed, so René Lalique continued to design many of the glass objects which were manufactured at the Combs la Ville and Wingen sur Moder factories. As he was now over seventy years old, not surprisingly his output no longer demonstrated the genius of his early years, although his artistic talents were still remarkable. He exhibited another glass fountain and a few commercial pieces at the 1937 Exposition Internationale des Arts et Techniques in Paris, but the designs were not greeted with the same enthusiasm as at earlier exhibitions: sadly, demand for decorative glass was on the decline.

Above: *A* motif décoratif *moulded with six chubby birds and designed to be used as a table decoration. Circa 1930. Length 28.7 cm 11 in*

Right: *A spectacular glass table made by Lalique in the 1930s. The circular top is moulded with* putti *dancing against a background of garlands of flowers. The central column was designed to be lit internally if desired. Height 66 cm 26 in. Diameter 87.5 cm 34$\frac{1}{4}$ in*

Panel made for Wanamaker's department store in Philadelphia

Chapter Four

GLASS IN ARCHITECTURE

Lalique was quick to realize that architecture and interior design were other spheres in which he could employ his unique talents with glass. His first major project, 40 Cours la Reine in Paris, for which he designed the façade, light fittings and furniture, was completed in 1902. Later the dazzling list was to include showrooms for Coty in New York; glass panels for the Compagnie des Wagon-Lits and fountains for the Champs Elysées; the light fittings and tableware for the first-class dining salon of the liner, the *S.S. Normandie,* and the exquisite furnishings for St Matthew's Church in Jersey.

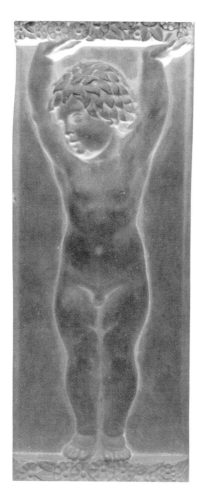

some of them were quite large, measuring up to 45 cm (18 inches) square. Lalique must have realized that architectural panelling of even larger proportions could prove a commercially viable aspect of his factory output.

One of the earliest commissions Lalique received for panel work was from François Coty, for the windows of his New York showroom on Fifth Avenue. These were installed around 1912 and can still be seen today. In 1926 the House of Worth also commissioned Lalique to design a façade for their Côte d'Azur premises in Cannes, which in the 1920s and 1930s was often called the playground of the world. This work, which included illuminated panels of frosted glass set in black marble, was a masterpiece of architectural design in the art deco style. Small rectangular panels of glass were incorporated into many pieces of art deco furniture as a decorative feature. The designs often bore sculpted relief work of swirling female nude forms, not unlike art nouveau motifs, while others had sunburst patterns of geometrically straight lines in the art deco manner.

Trains and ships
In the early 1920s Lalique had been asked to design some of the furnishings for the Compagnie des Wagons-Lits. He provided some panels in frosted glass

When Lalique designed the pine cone panelled glass doors for his Paris premises at 40 Cours la Reine in 1902, this prompted many commissions for similar work which continued throughout his distinguished career. The production of frosted glass plaques with moulded intaglio decoration had featured amongst his early glass productions – he had produced some small bas-relief glass pieces as early as 1890. They were usually framed in bronze and were clearly intended as *objets de vertu*, many of them being specially commissioned: interestingly,

Above: *Frosted glass panel made for the French President's car on the Côte d'Azur Pullman of the Compagnie des Wagon-Lits. 37 × 14 cm 14½ × 5½ in*

featuring female nudes against a background of fruiting vines in moulded relief. His finely executed panelling designs were featured on many of the French railways including the famous Côte d'Azur line.

The late 1920s and 1930s were also the age of the great passenger liners which cruised the oceans of the world. These floating palaces were the habitats of the world's richest people and they were opulent beyond the ordinary man's dreams. The French passenger liner *Paris*, launched in 1920, was advertised as one of the most luxurious and beautiful liners ever built, and Lalique was commissioned to design many of the ship's furnishings, including the light fittings and glass panelling. This was instantly successful, to wide acclaim, and many other commissions followed: the *Normandie, Ile de France, Empress of Britain* and the Swedish liner *Kungsholm* all provided ideal showcases for Lalique's work. He was commissioned to provide the light fittings for the massive first-class dining-room, designed by the architect Pierre Patout, on the *Ile de France*. These took the form of moulded rectangular ceiling tiles called *dalles*.

Lalique also supplied glass for the *Normandie*, one of the world's largest passenger liners, commissioned and launched in 1932. The first-class dining room was described in the ship's brochure as 'the largest room afloat', measuring over 91 metres (300 feet) in length. A contemporary drawing (see right) portrays the magnificence and splendour of its interior with panels of

Above: *An impression of the first class dining room on the liner,* Normandie, *launched in 1935. From a special edition of* L'Illustration, *published in June 1932*

rectangular ceiling lights and large vertical panels around the outside of the dining area, which also housed a dozen glass fountains, each with interior illumination. Sadly the liner was completely destroyed by fire in 1942 while at anchor in New York harbour, and many examples of works by France's greatest artists were lost forever.

Shops and hotels

Throughout the 1930s Lalique never lost an opportunity to exhibit his skill and craftsmanship in glass manufacture. He advertised widely and due to the worldwide acclaim he received from art and trade journals and newspaper reports, his work was always in demand and he was commissioned by many of the world's leading shops and hotels.

In 1925–6 the Arcades des Champs Elysées underwent a complete renovation and Lalique was asked to provide many of the illuminations and fountains. He made four identical large glass fountains for the Rond Point des Champs Elysées. These were greeted with enthusiasm by the Parisians, providing magnificent spectacles of light at night when they were illuminated from inside. They were circular in shape with the base covered in large sculpted pine cones. Sadly they were all destroyed during the Second World War.

Above: The glass panel, with the figures moulded in relief, which Lalique designed in 1932 to go above the wrought-iron lift doors at Claridge's Hotel in London

Lalique was also responsible for designing many smaller fountains for use in shop and arcade interiors. These were moulded in sections and often stood upon a basin made of mosaic-patterned glass to reflect the cascading water. Several had an octagonal panelled base containing a square central plinth of tapering design which supported a circular inverted glass bowl housing the lighting fixture which transmitted indirect light. Beneath this were four madonna-like figures.

Lalique's ingenuity in the use of back lighting for the illumination of wall panels, friezes and ceiling tiles, demonstrated at the 1925 Paris exhibition, led to architectural orders from the United States of America, where he was commissioned to design the interiors of shops and other buildings in New York and Los Angeles. Lalique was frequently referred to as the 'Luminary on Lighting' or the 'Magician of Light'.

Marc Lalique continued to be responsible for the outstanding commercial success of his father's innovations and he masterminded many of the campaigns for increased sales, particularly in the United States. Lalique had an impressive stand at the International Exhibition at Liège in Belgium in 1930 as well as a prominent display at the Ideal Home Exhibition run by the *Daily Mail* at Olympia, London in 1931 where he created a tremendous impression with another of his glass fountains. Claridge's Hotel in London used many of his glass panels moulded in relief with human figures to decorate doors and roofing areas as part of their renovations

Above: *Lalique's glass fountain designed for the main Ceramics Hall at the 1937 Exposition Internationale des Arts et Techniques in Paris*

to their interior decor. Examples of Lalique's glass panels may still be seen above the lift doors at Claridge's.

Church glass

It was at the 1930 Salon d'Automne exhibition in Paris that Lalique first exhibited one of his more unusual creations which once again emphasized his extraordinary versatility. This was a church altar constructed entirely of

panels of frosted glass, similar to a commission that Lalique had carried out at La Chapelle de la Vierge Fidèle in Caen in Normandy earlier that year. This was Lalique's first ecclesiastical work and in order to try to gain further commissions, examples of church architectural furnishings were exhibited at the Salon exhibitions of 1930 and 1931. However, it was not until 1933, at the exhibition at the Pavillon de Marsan, that Lalique revealed the full scale of his venture into church decoration. There was an enormous reredos with carved figures of six angels and a very large

panelled altar with a rail decorated in a superb pattern of lilies. The entire exhibit was made from panels of frosted glass.

The Pavillon de Marsan exhibition was instrumental in gaining Lalique his second church commission which is still intensely admired by all who see it, and considered one of his major works.

For some years Lalique had owned a villa in the South of France where he became a friend of Mrs Jesse Boot, who owned a neighbouring villa, and for which he designed two glass panelled doors. When Lalique later showed his ecclesiastical architectural glass at the Paris exhibition, Mrs Boot, now Lady Trent and living in Jersey, was so impressed that she decided to commission him to design and make the furnishings for St Matthew's Church at Millbrook, near St Helier in Jersey. As this church had for some time been in need of restoration and renovation and had a very plain interior, Lady Trent thought refurbishment would be a fitting tribute to her late husband, the first Lord Trent, and this was carried out in conjunction with the British architect A. B. Grayson in 1934.

St Matthew's Church

This was the largest church architectural commission that Lalique ever undertook. The visitor to St Matthew's Church first becomes aware that he is about to witness an astonishing work of art when he reaches the outer vestibule of the main nave. Here a large double door features two enormous vertical panels, each with a frosted glass figure of an angel over 2 metres (almost 7 feet) high, hands held together in prayer. The angel's robes fall in four panels of fluted folds, and each head is crowned with an arch of feathers simulating wings. Set within the walls of the vestibule are two Lalique figure sculptures standing within square frames.

On entering the nave of the church,

Above: *The holy-water glass font by Lalique at St Matthew's Church, Millbrook in Jersey was considered to be ultra-modern in the 1930s*

the full majesty, splendour and artistry that René Lalique lavished upon this commission can be fully appreciated. The central, predominating feature is an enormous glass cross over 3 metres (15 feet) high, sculpted in relief with Jersey lilies. On either side of the cross is a glass pillar, also heavily sculpted with lilies and over $3\frac{1}{2}$ metres (11 feet) high. These are all situated behind the main altar which is also made out of glass panels. The communion rails are formed of two sections of glass, each comprising five vertical panels, with each upper square bearing a moulded sculpture of two lilies, symmetrically placed and in full flower to symbolize purity.

The sanctuary and chancel are formed by four glass screens, each placed at right angles to the altar and consisting of nine vertical rectangular glass columns, crowned at the top by the same lily pattern seen in the communion rail decoration.

The two screens placed to the right of the main altar form the vestry, whilst those to the left enclose the Lady Chapel. In this side chapel is another altar made entirely of plain glass panels, above which stands the reredos screen with four sculpted angels, each over 3 metres (10 feet) in height. Their arms are crossed and their shoulders carved upon fluted corinthian columns with etched robed decoration at the side of each column. Their heads are crowned with winged feather decoration forming a dome over each angel's head. These angels have a beautiful simplicity and in no way detract from the act of worship. They are masterpieces executed in the very finest taste.

The tall side windows and light fittings in the nave are all made from Lalique glass panelling crowned at the top with Madonna lilies, many in full flower. The font has a square base with a rounded fluted column supporting the circular basin, which has a frieze pat-tern, heavily carved in straight arrow lines pointing upwards to form a continuous zigzag pattern around the rim of the font. The base is marked 'R. Lalique'. The sculpted shape and relief carving of this font were ultra-modern in the 1930s and although bearing art deco characteristics are totally in keeping with modern church architecture. It does not seem out of place today.

Glass Church

The whole body of the church is lit by enormous light troughs which cover the ceiling of the nave. All the fittings are of Lalique glass. During services the Great Cross behind the altar and the two supporting pillars on either side are illuminated, along with the striking group of four angels towering behind and atop the Lady Chapel altar. This creates a dazzling effect, particularly at night. The luminescent colours created by Lalique in his use of contrasting opaque and clear glass are amazing. It is no wonder that St Matthew's is often referred to as the 'Glass Church'.

The whole of this commission, as executed, is itself an outstanding tribute to the memory of René Lalique and has been and continues to be visited by many thousands of admirers for this reason. It will stand as a monument to the master for many future generations.

Opposite: Lalique's glass reredos screen in the Lady Chapel at St Matthew's Church, Jersey. Height 180 cm 70 in. It is made of glass with a satin finish. The fourth angel is hidden from view in this picture

'Hirondelles' (Swallows). This vase was made in 1920. Height 15.7 cm 6¼ in

Chapter Five

CIRE PERDUE

Throughout his life until arthritis crippled his hands, Lalique used the *cire perdue* (lost wax) technique to make unique one-off pieces of glass. They include vases, plaques, statuettes, ashtrays and hanging light fittings and all are distinguished by a roughly textured, frosted surface and the marks of the artist's fingerprints. Examples of *cire perdue* glass were made as display pieces for exhibitions, to special commission and as gifts for friends and colleagues, consequently they are very scarce and fetch extremely high prices – sometimes well into five figures – on their rare appearances in the salerooms.

From its earliest days Lalique glass was recognized as highly collectable. Even the many pieces of functional glass which were manufactured in their thousands at the Wingen factory feature in glass collections of today. Most of René Lalique's vases are eagerly snapped up at auctions and the rare snuff bottles and car mascots fetch high sums. Nevertheless one type of Lalique glass ranks as particularly desirable for the wealthy collector: the *cire perdue* glass.

Cire perdue, the 'lost wax' process of producing creations in glass (see page 53), has a special individuality. *Cire perdue* articles are fewer in number than those made by press-moulding techniques, which makes them all the more collectable. Competition at auction

sales is fierce, for Lalique glass pieces made by the *cire perdue* method are extremely valuable, being unique. Almost all of them were available only by special commission, or were displayed at glass exhibitions, where they were purchased by Lalique's wealthiest clients.

The earliest *cire perdue* works Lalique produced were small, solid statuettes. He only made a few of these and they belong to the latter part of his jewellery phase. They were intended as *objets de vertu* and sold purely for decorative

Above: *A very dramatic* cire perdue *vase, circa 1905. Height 12 cm 4¾ in. It is moulded with a design of three large moths with their wings outstretched*

purposes. Most of these statuettes are now to be found in museums, or in the great private collections of Lalique glass and jewellery. They therefore rarely appear on the market.

The first *cire perdue* vessels made as hollow containers are thought to have been produced around 1909 or 1910 and continued to be made until the late 1920s. A great many of these pieces exhibit characteristics which closely resemble Lalique's jewellery designs and occasionally a Japanese influence may be observed in the use of animal and insect sculpting on the grotesque, arresting designs. A small vase in the Calouste Gulbenkian Collection in Lisbon is a typical example. The body of the vessel is covered with flying moths and bats, their wings outspread and overlapping, their heads and appendages clearly modelled. This is a classic combination of the art nouveau style typically found in much of Lalique's early jewellery and the Japanese influence which is clearly in evidence. Another of his earliest *cire perdue* vases in the Calouste Gulbenkian Collection is known as the 'Medusa Vase'. This is 23 cm (9 inches) in height, with four Medusa heads of heavily patinated pink glass which protrude quite prominently around the body of the vase, giving a frighteningly realistic, grotesque effect. Each gorgon has an open mouth and is surrounded by four snakes encompassing a number of naked human forms, writhing as though in agony. The whole creation conveys a repugnant feeling of horror. Nevertheless this vase, though not perhaps to everyone's taste, is an

Above: *A* cire perdue *statuette of a woman. Circa 1901–05. Height 44 cm 17⅜ in. The figure has long hair and is swathed in leafy tendrils. It has a sepia patine and the facial features are lightly painted*

Overleaf (left): *A slender ovoid* cire perdue *vase with a design of trailing branches of ivy. Height 16 cm 6⅜ in*

Overleaf (right): *A* cire perdue *vase with a design of milk thistles. Height 20.4 cm 8 in*

Above: The macabre 'Medusa Vase', a cire perdue *piece from the Calouste Gulbenkian Museum in Lisbon which is described on page 117. Height 23 cm 9 in*

extraordinary work of art and an outstanding example of Lalique's early *cire perdue* glass work.

He also sculpted some hanging light fittings by the 'lost wax' process. An example of his more exotic work in this context is also to be found in the Gulbenkian Museum. This has a diameter of around 30 cm (12 inches) and is composed of numerous garden flowers, including daisies, hydrangeas and lilies. The flower-heads form a crowded design highlighted with a reddish-brown patina.

Lalique produced and designed many other *cire perdue* vases and statuettes over the years for exhibition purposes and it is interesting to note that in 1919 they were given a mark which showed a number code and the year of manufacture. This is of particular interest to connoisseurs and collectors of Lalique's work, for it gives an indication of the number of *cire perdue* pieces he produced. It also means that it is incorrect to assume that all Lalique's *cire perdue* work was produced by the master's own hand, for it can be calculated that between sixty and seventy of certain items were produced in one year, an almost impossible number to have been the work of a single individual, even of the stature of René Lalique.

Among some of the rarest examples of *cire perdue* work are models which in several places clearly show the modeller's fingerprints, an indication of the amazing sculpting detail that may be obtained by the *cire perdue* method. A figure of a cougar crouching upon a rock, which was sold by Phillips, New York, had numerous fingerprint marks clearly visible on the base of the sculpture. These fingerprints have been referred to as those of Lalique himself, although some scholars, while not entirely discounting the theory, have expressed some doubt about this.

The majority of the *cire perdue* artefacts have distinct individual characteristics which distinguish them quite markedly from the press-moulded products. Most of the latter have a sharp outline and are polished, whereas the *cire perdue* objects are unpolished: if one runs a finger over the surface of the glass it feels rough.

After the Great War, Lalique's *cire perdue* glass designs began to take on a symmetry not evident in his earlier subjects. He began to design vases with pairs of budgerigars perched on branches of blossom around the shoulders, obviously forerunners of some of his press-moulded vases which also have these bird designs. There are some examples of these in the Calouste Gulbenkian Museum.

Below: *A vase cast by the* cire perdue *method showing a frieze of* putti *holding flowering branches. Height 33 cm 13 in. The date of this vase is unknown*

REFERENCE SECTION

R LALIQUE

(A) Engraved mark, found on objects made before 1930

R.L.ALIQUE
FRANCE

(B) Stencilled mark, made by sand-blasting

R LALIQUE
FRANCE

(C) Etched mark, found on pieces made between c.1925 to c.1935

R.LALIQUE   FRANCE

(D) Moulded mark, found in intaglio and relief. Marks with good definition are generally produced by power press

Unlike his jewellery pieces, which were not always marked, almost all Lalique's glass products bear the mark 'R. Lalique' in various forms. The signature appears mostly in capital letters which are incised, engraved (A), stamped, stencilled (B) or wheel-cut (C), on or around the base of the glass artefact. The mark is not always easily visible and the piece has often to be held up to the light, especially when the signature is placed amongst the design decoration.

Sometimes the name 'Lalique' is press-moulded or blown-moulded upon the base (D), (E), (F) and (G). Sometimes the bottom line of the initial letter 'L' extends below the length of the name; this is known to collectors as the 'extended L' mark (H) and appears on the bases of some scent bottles and vases. As we have seen, scent bottles also have an etched or engraved pattern number on the bottom which corresponds with the number placed upon the base of the stopper. This is a useful guide to collectors in enabling them to ascertain that no exchange of stoppers has taken place.

After 1919 almost all Lalique *cire perdue* models, as well as having 'Lalique' or 'R Lalique France' marked on or around their bases, had a serialized number which ran consecutively from 'I' upwards, followed by a dash and

(E) Moulded mark. This type of mark, which has less clear definition than (D), appears on hand-blown pieces

(F & G) Moulded marks, with double-tailed Q

(H) Extended L mark. Relatively uncommon

R. Lalique

(I) Script signature, found on small objects

R. Lalique France N⁰ 3152

(J) Script signature, usually found on hand-blown pieces

two more numbers. These last two gave the year of manufacture. This is extremely useful in distinguishing Lalique's early *cire perdue* work from that of the 1920s. Marks on some work, from around 1914 on, had a script signature of 'R Lalique' (I) and (J), sometimes with the 'R' omitted. These marks were also put on his larger pieces of glass jewellery.

As the years progressed to the late 1920s, the word 'France' or the phrase 'Made in France' often appeared after the Lalique signature. When Lalique died in 1945, the 'R' was thereafter omitted from the signature. Unfortunately it is fairly easy for a forger to add an 'R' to a Lalique signature, thus making a spurious mark, intimating that the glass was made at an earlier date. Indeed, many hundreds of fake Lalique marks have appeared, over the years, on glass manufactured abroad as well as in France.

To serious collectors of Lalique glass, marks are of secondary interest and the prime consideration should be the design, the crispness of sculpture and the colour, which are the true hallmarks of the *maître verrier*. Fortunately, Lalique's skills are almost always immediately discernible by the collector with specialist knowledge. Nevertheless one should be constantly aware that as prices for genuine René Lalique glass continue to rise, so forgers will do their utmost to deceive the unwary.

The marks reproduced here are shown smaller than actual size.

COLLECTIONS

Many leading museums worldwide have exhibits of René Lalique's work. The largest collection of his jewellery, *objets de vertu* and glass is housed in the Calouste Gulbenkian Museum, Av. de Berna 45A, Lisbon, Portugal. In London his work can be seen at the Victoria & Albert Museum, SW7. Several pieces of his exotic jewellery are on view in the Anderson Collection, which is housed in the Sainsbury Centre for Visual Arts at the University of East Anglia in Norwich, Norfolk.

Most British provincial museums have a few examples of Lalique glass in their collections, while his wares make fairly regular appearances at the leading auction houses. Bonhams of Montpelier Street, London, SW7, have regular auction sales devoted exclusively to Lalique jewellery and glassware.

Examples of Lalique's exotic jewellery and fine glass have been purchased by the following museums.

UNITED STATES OF AMERICA
The Metropolitan Museum of Art
    (Lillian Nassau Collection)
Fifth Avenue
New York, New York 10028

The Museum of Fine Arts
Boulevard and Grove Avenue
Richmond
Virginia

FRANCE
Musée des Arts Décoratifs
107 rue de Rivoli
Paris 75001

WEST GERMANY
Museum für Kunst und Gewerbe
Steintorplatz
Hamburg 2000

Schmuckmuseum Pforzheim im
    Reuchlinhaus
Jahnstr. 42
Pforzheim 7530

AUSTRIA
Österreichisches Museum für
    angewandte Kunst
Stubenring 5
Vienna 1010

DENMARK
The Danish Museum of Decorative Art
Bredgade 68
1260 Copenhagen K

BIBLIOGRAPHY

Books

Arwas, Victor
Art Nouveau to Art Deco
London, 1987

Bayer, Patricia and Waller, Mark
The Art of René Lalique
London, 1988

Dawes, Nicholas M.
Lalique Glass
London, 1986

Duncan, Alastair
Art Nouveau and Art Deco Lighting
London, 1978

Klamkin, Marian
Collector's Book of Art Nouveau
Newton Abbot, 1971

Klein, Dan
All Colour book of Art Deco
London, 1974

Percy, Christopher Vane
The Glass of Lalique
New York, 1977

Savage, George
Glass and Glassware
London, 1973

Warren, Geoffrey
Art Nouveau
London, 1972

Articles in Periodicals

Becker, Vivienne
'Animals in Jewellery'
Collectors Guide, 1980

Farrar, J. Howard
'The Essence of Haute Couture'
Collectors Guide, 1985

Munn, Geoffrey
'René Lalique and Japanese Art'
The Antique Collector, 1987

Scarisbrick, Diana
'Tiaras – Floral and Leafy'
The Antique Collector, 1987

Scarisbrick, Diana
'Triumphant Evocation – Lalique
    Jewellery'
Country Life, 1987

The Studio,
various issues

Exhibition Catalogues

Art Nouveau, The Anderson Collection, Sainsbury Centre for Visual Arts, University of East Anglia, Norwich, 1980

The Jewellery of René Lalique (compiled by Vivienne Becker), Goldsmiths' Company, London, 1987

INDEX

ACKNOWLEDGEMENTS

All René Lalique material is reproduced with the permission of DACS, 1989.

The publishers would like to thank the following for their kind permission to reproduce the illustrations in this book:

Bonhams, London/Thomas Ward: endpapers, 6, 19, 45, 50, 53, 57, 67, 72 right, 73, 85 left, 88, 95 top, 97 right, 98, 99, 100 right, 106, 119; The Bridgeman Art Library: 4, 20, 64, 65, 72 left, 78 right, 115; The British Museum, London/The Hull-Grundy Bequest: 27; Christie's, London: 23, 42, 58, 59, 60, 62, 63, 70, 71, 80, 82, 83; Claridge's, London/Thistle Photography: 108; The Corning Museum of Glass, Corning, New York: 9, 51, 104, 121; Nicholas M. Dawes Collection, New York/Terry McGinnis, New York: 68; The Danish Museum of Applied Art, Copenhagen/Ole Woldbye: 22; J. Alastair Duncan: 18, 38 left, 85 right, 87, 91, 92, 97 left/David Weinstein Collection: 81; Mary Evans Picture Library: 107; Galerie Moderne/Andrew Stewart: 7, 8, 17, 55, 56, 61, 66, 74, 75, 76, 78 left, 79, 89, 95 bottom, 96, 100 left, 118; Calouste Gulbenkian Foundation (Lisbon): 16, 31 left, 37 top, 39, 41, 120/Reindaldo Viegas: 11, 12, 14, 24, 25, 30, 31 right, 33, 37 bottom, 40, 43, 44; John Jesse and Irina Laski Ltd: 34, 69; Michael Holford: 28, 29; Institut Français d'Architecture, Paris: 109; The Metropolitan Museum of Art (1985): 49; Musée d'art et d'histoire, Geneva/Musée de l'horlogerie et de l'emaillerie: 32; The National Motor Museum, Beaulieu, 21, 77; Rapho/Rega: 113; Phillips, New York: 105; Roger-Viollet: 15, 54, 94, 101; Sotheby's, London: 2, 26, 38 right, 52, 84, 86, 90, 93 left and right, 102, 103, 114, 116; St Matthew's Church, St Helier, Jersey: 110, 111; The University of East Anglia/The Anderson Collection: 46, 47; Mark Waller/Marvin Kagan Collection: 117.

Special thanks are due to The Revd. C. L. L. Binder, Vicar of St Matthew's Church, Millbrook, Jersey, C.I., for information on St Matthew's Church.